Morgan Lloyd Malcolm
Plays 1

T0348003

Margins and Marginality
Part I

Morgan Lloyd Malcolm
Plays 1

Belongings
The Wasp
Mum
When the Long Trick's Over
The Passenger

With an introduction by
MORGAN LLOYD MALCOLM

methuen | drama
LONDON • NEW YORK • OXFORD • NEW DELHI • SYDNEY

METHUEN DRAMA
Bloomsbury Publishing Plc
50 Bedford Square, London, WC1B 3DP, UK
1385 Broadway, New York, NY 10018, USA
29 Earlsfort Terrace, Dublin 2, Ireland

BLOOMSBURY, METHUEN DRAMA and the Methuen Drama logo are trademarks
of Bloomsbury Publishing Plc

First published in Great Britain 2023

Introduction copyright © Morgan Lloyd Malcolm, 2023
The Wasp copyright © Morgan Lloyd Malcolm, 2015
Belongings copyright © Morgan Lloyd Malcolm, 2011
Mum copyright © Morgan Lloyd Malcolm, 2021
When the Long Trick's Over copyright © Morgan Lloyd Malcolm, 2022
The Passenger copyright © Morgan Lloyd Malcolm, 2023

Morgan Lloyd Malcolm has asserted her right under the Copyright, Designs and
Patents Act, 1988, to be identified as author of this work.

Cover image © Badr Safradi/Getty Images

All rights reserved. No part of this publication may be reproduced or transmitted
in any form or by any means, electronic or mechanical, including photocopying,
recording, or any information storage or retrieval system, without prior
permission in writing from the publishers.

Bloomsbury Publishing Plc does not have any control over, or responsibility for,
any third-party websites referred to or in this book. All internet addresses given
in this book were correct at the time of going to press. The author and publisher
regret any inconvenience caused if addresses have changed or sites have
ceased to exist, but can accept no responsibility for any such changes.

Applications for performance of *Belongings*, *Mum* and *The Wasp*, including readings
and excerpts, throughout the world by amateurs in the English language (except in the
United States of America and Canada) should be made before rehearsals begin to Nick
Hern Books, The Glasshouse, 49a Goldhawk Road, London W12 8QP, tel + 44 (0)20
8749 4953, e-mail rights@nickhernbooks.co.uk. Applications for performance by
professionals in any medium and in any language throughout the world, and for
amateur performances of *The Passenger* and *When the Long Trick's Over* should be
addressed to The Haworth Agency, e-mail info@haworthagency.co.uk. All rights
whatsoever in these plays are strictly reserved. No performance may be given unless a
licence has been obtained, and no alterations may be made in the title or the text of
the play without the author's prior written consent. No rights in incidental music or
songs contained in the work are hereby granted.

A catalogue record for this book is available from the British Library.

A catalog record for this book is available from the Library of Congress.

ISBN: PB: 978-1-3504-2432-6
       ePDF: 978-1-3504-2433-3
       eBook: 978-1-3504-2434-0

Series: Contemporary Dramatists

Typeset by RefineCatch Limited, Bungay, Suffolk

To find out more about our authors and books visit www.bloomsbury.com
and sign up for our newsletters.

Contents

Introduction

What an honour this is! If you could tell seventeen-year-old Morgan that one day I would have a *Plays One* on the shelves of bookshops I genuinely think she would have not believed it. It was at that age that I was scrabbling around trying to find plays to perform with girlfriends as part of my A-Level Theatre Studies course. I ended up doing a version of the *Dumb Waiter* by Harold Pinter with my mate and we played them as men and loved every second of it. We had been desperate to do something that was dark and funny and let us show off our strengths in a way that we couldn't find in the other play texts that were available in the late nineties. We wanted to play complicated and morally ambiguous characters. We wanted to play proper humans with a myriad of impulses and behaviours. Play texts really weren't too available and this play was the one that hit all the marks for us. We had a blast.

It was years later, when I was trying to work out what to write, that I remembered this feeling and embarked on writing my own two hander that could be performed by women and contain two-characters who had all the layers I'd been searching for as a seventeen-year-old. *The Wasp* was the result of this. And not to say there aren't many many plays that hit that mark out there but I think, when I was starting to establish myself as a playwright, I realised that maybe one of the things I could do in my capacity as a woman writer with dark and funny and complex impulses is try to focus on those kinds of characters. Essentially, when I started out writing I was very aware of the huge selection of phenomenal roles for men and, in particular, was watching a lot of my actress mates struggle to get work and I decided that perhaps a useful thing I could do was to start writing more roles for women. So this is what I did.

My first play was *Belongings*, which emerged out of this very impulse. In fact I think it came directly from a conversation with the actress and my great friend, Katie Lyons, who was struggling for roles at the time. I told her I'd write her a part. I embarked on an intense and fascinating research mission around women in the army, and the depictions of women in society, and themes of belonging and identity and what emerged was this play that would be a huge challenge for a central performer to get their teeth into. In the end, when we got programmed at the Hampstead Theatre downstairs, Katie got a role in a BBC comedy playing another soldier and couldn't join us but that initial spark of simply wanting to create some jobs for women is, to this day, my greatest energiser.

Before I wrote *Belongings* I had been working for many years writing and performing comedy with Katie and our co-writer Verity Woolnough. I ended up giving up performing as I realised I was finding it terrifying and preferred writing. I went on to write several pantos, Christmas shows, community shows and site specific immersive shows; most of which were team written. *Belongings* was my first attempt at writing on my own. What I discovered was that, when I wrote on my own, I slipped into a darker mode. I couldn't quite let go of the comedy but I was definitely finding a more tragic path to take. Perhaps this is the vibe of every first-time writer, mining their psyche for the dark stuff, or perhaps it was just born of a certain frustration at the gender inequalities and violences I was witnessing at the time. Whatever it was, I really wanted to write something that asked proper questions about gender identity and violence against women. This became another spark for me. If I am given a stage – what do I wish to say? What can I say?

Next came *The Wasp* and, as mentioned before, I was hoping to write something really knotty and dark and funny in a way that I had failed to find as a seventeen-year-old. But I was also in the midst of first-time parenthood and I was drowning a bit. I wrote that play in my head as I walked my wakeful baby round South East London. I essentially engaged with the proper planning of a play in a way I had never done before and was surprised to learn how much it worked! As a professional procrastinator I had never fully clocked the benefit of planning thoroughly before that. As I walked, I thought of the characters, mapped out their lives, got to know how they spoke, imagined them in different scenarios. I then put them together, often speaking to them as I pushed the pram through parks and up roads. I got to the point where I couldn't do anything except write. I knew them inside out by the time I sat at my laptop. The play flowed out easily.

The first act was originally a short play for a festival. The feedback was – what happens next? So I did more walking and then wrote the second and third act in a weekend. As I wrote I knew someone would have to die but I didn't know who until I wrote it. The work I had done on those characters was so intensive it meant I could simply let them speak. It was a revelation to me to be honest. It totally changed the way I worked. My tiny baby had forced me into a scenario where I had to learn a new way. I couldn't just wing it anymore. I didn't have time to. And if I planned it all out, knew everything about my characters, then in those moments I did have time to write, it would flow. I'm not saying it has always worked perfectly ever since but it was an important lesson for this particular playwright who tends to leave everything to the last minute.

It was several years later that I wrote *Mum*, which had a very scenic route to the stage but was eventually picked up by producer Francesca Moody and director Abigail Graham who were the first ones who really understood what it was I was grappling with in it. Those many months of walking the streets with my first born had been tough. I struggled with early parenthood. My experience was a dark one (which perhaps explains a lot of the violence of *The Wasp*) and, when I finally tried to channel it into a piece, it became something that was its own beast. From an initial prompt of 'what scares you the most in the whole world' came the answer 'having my children taken from me because someone thinks I've done something terrible to them'.

It's a nasty and horrible thought. It was a huge challenge to write. The research I did into the Family Court system and court cases involving child abuse and injury was tough. But I also wanted to make sure I was addressing a very real fear that was rooted in something I had experienced – post-natal anxiety and intrusive thoughts. The experience of an intrusive thought can be an all consuming horror played out in your head in the blink of an eye but it has a very real, physical and emotional affect on you. *Mum* was my chance to try and articulate this. It was a tough play to make and to watch but, for the parents who approached me afterwards: I wrote it for you as well as me.

Another play that had a pretty circuitous route to the stage is *When the Long Trick's Over* . . . which is an example of how something can begin in one place and end up somewhere else. It was part of a commission via the Soho Theatre that never made it to their stage for one reason or another. It was then picked up by Rowan Rutter and High Tide made it happen. I will remain eternally grateful it finally got its chance but we were also very unlucky to have produced it just as the Covid pandemic was still spiking. It went on a tour of the East of England that was very interrupted by cancelled performances and the phenomenal cast didn't get a chance for a proper run at it.

This play, about grief and endurance and the human body and what it's capable of, was born of my own experiences of death and how I found relief in swimming. It has become one of those plays that I wrote at a very specific time in my life and is almost a time capsule of those moments. It was put on almost six years after I wrote it so it was quite a surreal and fascinating experience as it felt like stepping back in time a little, or looking through an old photo album. I am so glad I wrote it and that it was finally staged. I wish we had been able to have a longer, fuller run of it.

Finally I am so glad to be able to include a short monologue that was written as a Globe Theatre commission for a ghost story night they ran. *The Passenger* is a creepy little story that draws on my own experiences of the paranormal and plays on the fun of telling a proper ghost story. The conceit of it is designed to make the audience think that anything can happen and it is also possible to perform this in a very lo-fi way. All you need is an actor to read it and some well timed off-stage bangs and screams!

I went on to revive it as part of the very first Terrifying Women show. Formed with Abi Zakarian, Sampira and Amanda Castro, the Terrifying Women nights are a chance to nurture and develop horror for the stage written by women and non-binary writers. It's become a haven for a new way of working that favours kindness and compassion but also a place to try and write about the things the scare and unsettle us. It's a cathartic and fun chance to get a bunch of very talent humans together to scare the bejesus out of an audience. *The Passenger* was part of the first incarnation of this and is still my favourite of my ghost stories. Maybe because some of it is true. I won't say which bits.

I hope that was a useful overview of the plays contained in this collection. I am proud of each and every one of them. Much like children, I cannot pick a favourite, but I am thrilled that they have all been collected together like this. When I look at this particular selection I can really track through a need of mine to write plays that provide fun and meaty roles for women and to tackle the themes and issues that were impacting me at the time of writing. What an honour to have been able to find a way to do this in this life. I will never stop feeling grateful that I've somehow managed to make writing my job. It's an honour to be able to channel my own experiences and explore the world in this way.

But I also love the form of theatre and its possibilities for making real change happen. I hope that some of what I have written is useful to you and the people you perform it with and for. Because plays are lovely to read but really they're written to be performed. And when I'm feeling super sentimental I like to hope that there are seventeen-year-olds out there like I was, searching for something meaty to perform for their exam and finding in these pages characters and stories that they can really get their teeth into.

With love, Morgan
April 2023

Belongings

Morgan Lloyd Malcolm

When I originally wrote *Belongings* I understood there to be a feminist approach to depicting sexual violence that was one that insisted on us not shying away from the brutal truth of it. That it needed to be depicted fully and not shied away from. I was early on in my learning as a feminist and both misconstrued things and also didn't critically think it through enough. I was particular in my stage directions as a result.

I have since changed my opinion on this and instead believe that there is never a good reason to see a sexual assault depicted naturalistically. We have a duty of care to our audiences and to our performers and those who make our work.

I would like to urge anyone staging this play to take this into consideration when choreographing the moment of the assault. It is a trauma the character has suffered, but we don't need to see it to understand what has happened. Thankfully in theatre there are many ways we can find to depict or imply it in a manner that will not be retraumatising for those performing and watching. I hope this opens up greater possibilities for you than a naturalistic reconstruction would.

Morgan x

Belongings was first performed at Hampstead Theatre, London, on 19 May 2011. The production extended to Trafalgar Studios on 16 June 2011. The cast was as follows:

Jim	Ian Bailey
Deb	Joanna Horton
Jo	Kirsty Bushell
Sarko	Calum Callaghan

Creative Team

Writer: Morgan Lloyd Malcolm
Director: Maria Aberg
Designer: Naomi Dawson
Lighting: David Holmes
Sound: Carolyn Downing
Production Manager: Ed Wilson
Company Stage Manager: Sarah Cowen
Assistant Director: Sophie Ivatts

Scene One

A detached new build home in a cul-de-sac somewhere outside Chippenham. The kitchen. A room split in two by a sideboard that creates a dining area at one end, kitchen at the other. Evening. **Deb** *looks around the room – though it is her home, it has changed. Suddenly a completely naked man stomps in. This is* **Jim**. **Deb** *is positioned so that* **Jim** *doesn't notice her at first. He goes to a cupboard and is looking for something.* **Deb** *is finding it hard not to laugh and doesn't quite know whether to say something. Eventually* **Jim** *turns and sees* **Deb**. *He yelps out in fright. When they speak it is with Chippenham accents.*

Jim   FUCK!

He makes no attempt to cover his modesty.

Jim   Jesus H fuckin' christ Deb! You scared the livin' bejesus out of me you fuckin'! What the?! When d'you get back then? Fuck!

Deb   Just now.

Jim   I'd bloody hug you if I didn't have my nob out.

Deb   Yeh. About that, Dad . . .?

He grabs a tea towel and covers up.

Jim   What, your dad's gonads not good enough for you eh?

Deb   Er . . .

Jim   Fuckin' hell you're back!

Deb   Yeh I am.

Jim   I thought I was gonna pick you up?

Deb   Me too.

Jim   You never told me when though.

Deb   Yeh I did. But no matter. Honestly. Got the bus.

Jim   Got the fuckin' bus? Fucksake. Serve our country and got the bus. Sorry mate.

Deb   Honestly don't stress.

Jim   Well I knew it would be today or tomorrow or somethin' I just didn't know the exact time.

Deb   Seriously. Don't.

Jim   Well. Look atchoo. Jo's gonna be stoked. Seriously. She's been plannin' your return dinner for weeks.

Deb   I don't want a fuss.

Jim   Why not?! Almost two years you dickhead.

Deb   Make that a year and a half.

Jim   You say potato. Oh mate. Not spent proper time with you in ages. Nice of you to bless us with your presence this time.

Deb   Don't start. You know I needed a holiday. A proper one.

Jim   Yeh I know. Glad to be home then?

Deb   Yeh.

Jim   Well I am. I'm glad you're home. All the shit in the papers about. Well. I'm glad you're in one piece. It would have been a fucker if you'd lost a limb eh? Got burnt or summat?

Deb   Better than dyin' though eh?

Jim   Is it? Complete change of lifestyle. Complete change to the way you live.

Deb   Yeh well. I had mates that we lost so. Maybe a drink?

Jim   Yeh you don't wanna be talkin' about this now eh? But I mean – we'd have had to convert this place for you. Do you get money to do that from the army? Do they sort you out with kit if you're disabled in combat and that?

Deb   Yeh I guess. Can I have a drink?

Jim   Help yourself. I doubt they'd completely help you though. I bet most of the burden lays on the family don't it? We'd be the ones left moppin' you up eh?

Deb   Yeh well I'm fine in-I? Can we leave it? Do you want one too?

Deb *has gone to the fridge and pulls out a couple of beers.*

Jim   Go on then.

Deb   All changed.

Jim   What's that then?

Deb   This place.

Jim   Jo did a rejig. Better aint it?

Deb   Yeh.

Jim   'cept the frogs. Fucking frogs everywhere. Jo loves her frogs.

Deb   Yeh I know.

Jim   Lick of paint. Scrubbed up alright.

Deb   What did you do with all mum's stuff then?

Jim   Who's that then?

Deb   Dad . . .

Jim   Yeh alright. Chucked it didenI?

Deb   Yeh.

Jim   Well I weren't gonna keep it was I? Erect a shrine? She aint dead.

Deb   She may as well be.

Jim   Yeh too right mate. 'If I never see her again' and all that.

Deb   Yeh. Jo alright is she?

Jim   Course she is. Life of riley that girl. Got it made.

Deb   Yeh you're really livin' the high life aintcha?

Jim   I aint heard her complainin'.

Deb   She's done a good job. Anyways. Would you mind puttin' some clothes on maybe?

Jim   I'd just had a shower see?

Deb   I don't want to know what you've been doin' thanks.

What were you lookin' for?

Jim   Fags.

Deb   In the kitchen cupboard?

Jim   Jo's been hidin' them. Tryin' to get me to stop.

Deb   Is it working?

Jim   Is it fuck.

Deb *gets a pack of fags out and offers him one.*

Deb   Here y'are.

Jim   Hold that thought. I'll be back after I made meself decent.

Deb   Gonna take more than clothes to achieve that.

Jim   Cheeky bastard.

Jim *leaves.* **Deb** *lights her fag and drinks her beer. She surveys the room. The sound of the front door opening and closing and then* **Jo** *enters. She is a few years older than* **Deb**. *She is carrying shopping bags which she drops as soon as she sees* **Deb**.

Jo   Deb! Oh! Whendyou get in then? Whendyou arrive? Oh!

C'mere!

She embraces **Deb** *who awkwardly and stiffly reciprocates, still holding her fag and beer.*

Deb   No worries. Just now didenI?

Jo   What a massive surprise you sneak! Your dad didn't know when you'd be ready for pickup. We didn't know when to expect you. I'm sorry Deb.

Deb   Don't worry mate honestly. How are you?

Jo   Oh I'm fine but what about you? Look at you! All tanned up. Been sunbathin' out there have you?

Deb   Can't really avoid it. Did quite a bit of my duties in my sports bra to be honest. It was over fifty degrees sometimes.

Jo   No! How can you do anythin' in that kind of heat?

Deb   You acclimatise.

Jo   You must have been drinkin' gallons of water a day.

Deb   Yeh.

Jo   Your dad and I were only sayin' the other day about this hot spell we're havin' that it probably isn't half as hot as where you were and we were bloody right then weren't we? I think we were somethin' like twenty-five degrees or summink! And there we were – all sparked out on the patio. Didn't get nuffin' done. Twenty-five degrees and we're no use to anyone.

Deb   Yeh?

Jo   Well you know your dad. Any excuse to just loll about. And then you're out there runnin' about in fifty degrees? You're like some action hero!

Deb   Yeh?

Jo   Super-Deb!

Deb   Well.

Jo   I got to get dinner goin' then!

Deb   I don't want a fuss, Jo.

Jo   Well tough tits you're gettin' one. A year and a half sweetheart. A year and a half. How long we got you for?

Deb   Don't know.

Jo   Well how long's your leave?

Deb   I aint goin' back.

Jo   Serious?

Deb   Yeh well. Done my time aint I?

Jo   Yes you bloody have.

Deb   Yeh well.

Jo   C'mere.

Jo *grabs her and hugs her. This time* **Deb** *is less awkward. She pulls away quickly though.*

Deb   Alright calm down!

Jo   Really pleased love.

Deb   Yeh I get it.

Jo   I'm makin' lasagna! Where's your dad to?

Deb   He went to put some clothes on diden he?

Jo   Well won't that make a nice change? Why don't you go and get out of your kit? Get yourself comfy and I'll get goin' with the food.

Deb   I want to stay down here and help you out.

Jo   Well I want you to get settled back in. Relax.

Deb   Mate last time I saw you . . .

Jo   Don't. Now you shush-up and if you aint goin' upstairs then you can help me lay the table or something. Make a change from our laps. I've got some candles somewhere. And I definitely have a lighter so. Right. Onwards. Let's get dinner on the go.

Deb   I like what you did. With this place.

Jo   Yeh?

Deb   Different and that. But yeh. Made it yours.

Pause. Something passes between them. **Jim** *enters and notices the quiet.*

Jim   What, are we having a minute's silence in honour of the complete fuckin' lack of any dinner being cooked?!

Jo   I'm on it.

Jim   My daughter's home and I wanna celebrate! C'mere!

He grabs **Deb** *and bear hugs her and scrubs her head.*

Jim   Well done for not gettin' yourself disabled!

Deb   Fuck off, Dad!

Jim   I'm already runnin' more websites than I can keep a handle on. More of a strain on the old resources and it would have got well tight.

Deb *manages to extricate herself from his arms.*

Deb   Still changing the world with your business ideas then?

Jim   You know me sweetcheeks. Gis that fag then. And don't fuckin' look at me like that Jo – I'm celebratin' the return of my daughter.

Jo   I had my back to you Jim, I weren't lookin' anywhere near you.

Jim   Well I could feel you thinkin' it.

Jo   Thinkin' what?

Jim   Thinkin' up new ways to make my life a misery.

Jo   Well that's a nice way to speak to the woman who's makin' your dinner.

Jim   Well this is the man who's payin' for it. C'mon, Deb – gis that fuckin' fag.

Deb*, who has been hesitating as she listens to their conversation, takes a fag out of its packet and holds it out to* **Jim***. However as she does the Scene changes around her,* **Jim** *and* **Jo** *disappear and . . .*

Scene Two

. . . We transition into the desert. The past.

Evening. **Deb** *is still holding out her fag and* **Sarko** *enters, taking it from her. We're in the sleeping quarters. It's a big tent in which* *six soldiers are housed – sleeping on camp beds that can be made private by mini-tents around them. Their belongings hang in clothes tidies and sit in plastic boxes under their beds and posters adorn the walls – including several topless women. We only need see* **Deb** *and* **Sarko**'s *beds.* **Sarko** *is holding a bottle of shower gel that has had a cock and balls drawn on it with a marker pen.*

Sarko   Bored were you?

Deb   Someone got 'cocked'?

Sarko   Actin' all innocent.

Deb   What you lookin' at me for?

Sarko   'Cos you were the one that done it a billion times before!

Deb   Don't lie!

Sarko *grabs a plastic box of his stuff and holds up, one by one, his belongings that have been 'cocked'.*

Sarko   Shampoo! Hair gel! Face cream!

Deb   Vain bastard. You've got more toiletries than me.

Sarko   Oh this is one I aint seen before. My toothbrush? You twat! My toothbrush?! That's just fuckin' wrong.

He demonstrates brushing his teeth with the cock facing front. **Deb** *finds this hilarious.*

Deb   I'm a fuckin' genius!

Sarko   I can't use this no more!

Deb   It's like you're sucking a nob!

Sarko   Yeh yeh. Laugh it up. So glad to know we've got you protecting our country.

Deb   Oh like you're so pure.

She holds up her hairbrush which has also been cocked and brushes her hair with it.

Deb (*playacting*)   Oh I wanted to brush my hair but someone keeps poking me with their hard-on.

Sarko (*laughing*)   Idiot.

Moment of calm as they settle. **Sarko** *lights his fag.*

Sarko   Cooled down a bit now aint it?

Deb   Yeh.

More fiddling with stuff. **Sarko** *picks up a magazine. He sees that it has also been 'cocked'. He holds it up accusatorialy.*

Sarko   Really?

Deb   You were fuckin' ages in the shower.

Sarko   Even Maggie? Beautiful pure Maggie?

Deb   Who?

He holds up a picture in the magazine of Maggie Gyllenhaal who has been 'cocked'.

Deb   Oh yeh, I know.

Sarko   Would you?

Deb   Who her? Yeh. Definitely. You?

Sarko   Nah. But I tell you who I would . . .

He flicks through the magazine.

Sarko   There's my girl – Charlize Theron?

Deb   Let's have a look? Not for me, no.

Sarko   Really? Lindsay Lohan?

Deb   No. Do you know why? She'd be too eager to please.

Sarko   That's a good thing aint it?

Deb   No it aint. Complete turn off. Eager to please equals low self-confidence. No thanks. I don't want someone giving me the

porn star routine. All pantin' and 'ooohing'. I want genuine
reactions. Give me Maggie any day. I reckon she'd be awesome.

Sarko   Not enough tits for me.

Deb   Why, how many do you want?

Sarko   Yeh yeh.

Deb   It's not all about the tits.

Sarko   It is for me.

Deb   Not that I don't like a nice pair; it's just not all about them.

Sarko   Ah bless you Deb. You old romantic.

Deb   Oh whatever.

Sarko   No it's lovely.

Deb   Dick.

Sarko   Need a bit of romance in this place eh? Need a bit of
loveliness. This sandy. This sandy old. Pit. Of.

Pause.

Deb   You done then?

Pause. **Sarko** *is thinking.*

Sarko   I've got this theory about the desert.

Deb   Oh here we go . . .

Sarko   It's a place, right. That is stripped down to the very basics
of life. There's fuckin' barely anythin' here. There's nothin'.

Deb   Right . . .

Sarko   It's a barren wasteland of nothing-ness. Hot, arid, parched,
neglected.

Deb   Yeh . . .

Sarko   Bit like your bush.

Deb   Fuck off!

Sarko   But anything here of any use to us is man-made. But still – there's not quite nothin' is there?

Deb   You just said there's nothing here.

Sarko   Shuttup. Because you still get shrubs. Or trees dotted about. Still there are the odd signs of life.

Deb   Where are you going with this?

Sarko   And my eyes aren't interested in the man-made stuff. It's the bits of life that catch me. Because more often than not they're hiding something or someone that wants to kill me. In a place so empty of life; the only bits of it there are can potentially kill me. I'm including humans in this too by the way. We're fuckin' killin' each other in a place where life is fuckin' rare. It doesn't make sense. We should be holdin' on to whatever there is. We're an endangered species in the desert that's what we are.

A pause.

Deb   That's not a theory.

Sarko   What?

Deb   That's an observation you thick twat.

Sarko   What the . . .? Shut the fuck up I'm just tryin' to raise the fuckin' tone here.

Deb   You're what?

Sarko   Have an intelligent conversation. Get a bit fuckin' philosophical alright? Who are you? The pedantic fairy? Fuck off.

Deb   Easy up there Sark. Just puttin' my two pennies worth in.

Sarko   Well have it back. Next time I want a conversation I'll talk to that sandbag over there shall I? I'll get more respect from it.

Deb   Don't start a conversation like that if you don't want a response Sarko. Just because I disagree with you doesn't mean I don't want to talk about it. It's called a 'debate'.

Sarko   I know what it's called you patronising dick.

Deb   Oh look at you gettin' all puffed up like some rooster on steroids. Little prick – what's the problem?

Sarko   You are. Do you realise how high above the rest of us you place yourself? Notice that I said 'place yourself' because no one else has put you there. Just because you've made it out here with us it don't mean you're the queen of the fuckin' desert.

Deb   OK you're ravin' now.

Sarko   You're still only a soldier like the rest of us. A bunch of fuckin' reject idiots who had nothin' better to do with our lives that give them up for a fuckin' country who barely even knows we're out here. Barely even knows it.

Deb   Where the hell did that come from?! Is that what you actually think?

Sarko   Fuck off.

Deb   We're the best army in the world, mate. You know that.

We're the best. I'm proud of being part of it. I always wanted to be a soldier. I'm proud to be here and I'm glad I'm 'only' a soldier like the rest of us. And I'm gonna work my way up that ladder until I'm fuckin' Major if I can.

Sarko   I don't know what we're doin' here is all.

Deb   Do you care? It's our job, mate. And in my opinion we do it bloody well.

Sarko   Just sayin'.

Deb   Just sayin' what? Hot air. This place is gettin' to you is all. Why'd you go and put a downer on the evenin'? Man up, princess. This is our life.

Sarko   'Man up princess'?

Deb   Yeh.

They start cracking up. **Sarko** *starts to get into his bed . . .*

Sarko   'Man up princess'?!

Deb   Yeh! What? Fuckin' man up!

Sarko   You're a fuckin' dick you are.

Deb   Takes one to know one.

Sarko   Dick.

Deb   Yeh yeh.

Sarko (*from his bunk*)   So glad I'm stuck with you out here in . . . You cocked my pillow?! You cocked my fucking pillow?!

Deb   Sweet dreams asshole.

Sarko   You'd better watch your back mate. That's all I'm sayin'. You'd better watch your back.

Deb *chuckles to herself.*

Deb   Sweet dreams.

Scene Three

We are back in Chippenham. This time we're in **Jim***'s office which has been converted, badly, from a bedroom.*

Deb   Did you literally just move my bed and wardrobe and put your desk in here?

Jim   Pretty much.

Deb   You didn't want to re-decorate or nothin'?

Jim   I only use it for work.

Deb   Thanks by the way. Didn't wait long by the sounds of it.

Jim   Well if you will use your leave to go gallavantin' off on holiday rather than seein' your old man.

Deb   What? Come home and play at happy families?

Jim   Yeh well.

Deb   Go on then give me the info.

Jim   What?

Deb   Your business.

Jim   Oh now, what do you want to know?

Deb   How are you making money from this?

Jim   Simple. Check this out. They use my payment software and every time they use it I get a percentage.

Deb   So you get money for doing nothin' then?

Jim   Well it aint doin' nothin' when I've spent time developin' it is it? But yeh. I aint liftin' a finger once it's out there.

Deb   Thought people could pretty much get it all for free these days anyways? What mugs have you got payin' for it then?

Jim   Mugs who like the harder stuff. Weirder. I don't know.

Deb   Nice. My father, so proud, providin' them paedos with a well run service.

Jim   Shuttup it's not that kind of stuff. Bondage. Hardcore.

Bukake.

Deb   Do I want to know what Bukake is?

Jim   Take one Japanese woman and a bunch of Japanese guys and get them to jizz all over her face. Bukake.

Deb   What a nice image. Thanks, Dad.

Jim   Seriously mate. The stuff that's out there. Caters for all tastes. I aint sayin' I'm a punter but I'm tellin' you now this aint exactly the worst way to earn a livin' if you know what I mean.

Deb   Not your average nine to five.

Jim   You'd love it. Spend my day lookin' at tits and makin' creative decisions about which ones to feature. Fuckin' made mate.

Deb   So it's not just software you're into then?

Jim   Nah, you know me. I figured that if they were making cash from traffic to their sites and using my software to get the money

from them why don't I cut out the middle man and make some
sites of my own?

Deb   Where do you get your pictures from and that?

Jim   Just rip them from other sites. Easy enough.

Deb   You got it all sewn up aintcha? Fingers in all the pies.

Jim   I wish.

Deb   And you aint got no problem bein' in this business?

Jim   Why should I? Oldest profession in the world.

Deb   Thought that was prostitution?

Jim   Look. They get paid well. There are legislations and that.
They choose it. And it is merely providin' a public service. People
need to let off steam. Relax. Why, why am I even sayin' all this?
Are you some kind of moral police all of a sudden? Do I need to
tell you what it is you do for a livin'?

Deb   What? Protect our country?

Jim   Nah – kill people.

Deb   Bit more to it than that.

Jim   Is there? It's all violence at the end of the day. Hurtin'
people. Gettin' power over people. We're in the same business
mate.

Deb   I fuckin' hope not.

Jim   Do you know what your problem is? You're livin' in a
bubble. The life you lead aint real. You're looked after. Fed.
Watered. Clothed. Told where to go and what to do. You're not
makin' any decisions for yourself. You 'ant no idea what it's like to
be a real human being because you're a robot. And you're a
miserable robot aren't you, Deb?

You're not happy. I can tell. And you won't be until you let go and
admit you're an animal like the rest of us. Then maybe we can talk.

A pause.

Jim   What?

Deb *leaves the room and we transition into the kitchen.*

Scene Four

The kitchen. It's later in the evening of **Deb**'s *arrival, after dinner.*
Jo *has finished tidying up.* **Jim** *is in his office off.* **Deb** *is making
tea for* **Jo** *and herself.*

Deb   So I'm thinkin' I'll get a job and that. I don't know.

Somethin' simple for a while. Settle back.

Jo   Good luck!

Deb   Get myself a place, see whether I could live round here
again. I don't know.

Jo   You don't need a place.

Deb   Reckon it would be good to get back into the old routines.

Jo   Thought army was job for life and that?

Deb   Would be nice to have a bit of normality for once.

Jo   Careful what you wish for mate.

Deb   Have you seen any of the old lot recently?

Jo   No.

Deb   Not out at pub then?

Jo   Ant been for a while.

Deb   Fancy goin'?

Jo   Now?

Deb   Yeh.

Jo   Nah.

Deb   Why not?

Jo   Got things to do.

Deb   Got what?

Jo   Got a wash on. Got to hang it out. I'm tired anyway.

Deb   You're a barrel of laughs now aintcha?

Jo   Yeh well. Aint really been there since. Well, since you were here last. When we were. At that New Year party.

Deb   Oh man.

Jo   Dancin' like twats.

Deb   Speak for yourself.

Jo   Nickin' vodka from behind the bar.

Deb   Last ones standin' at the lock-in.

Jo   Standin'? Don't think so.

Deb   Yeh.

Slight pause.

Deb   Remember summer after your A Levels?

Jo   A level. Just the one.

Deb   Right laugh weren't it?

Jo   Yeh.

Deb   Down the river with the lads. What happened to Craig then? Ant seen him since school.

Jo   Oh blimey. Got some girl from Frome pregnant, got married, got divorced, got a job in Bristol, DJs in some pub out there on thursdays and likes pictures of motorbikes.

Deb   How the fuck do you know all that?

Jo   Facebook.

Deb   Oh I see. You don't go to the pub but you make sure you keep up with what everyone's doin'? Like some internet stalker? You're no better than dad.

Jo   Piss off I am. And I don't know what pub you're talkin' about because no one goes down the Bell no more.

They've all buggered off. All them lot I know what they're doin' now though. Kerry has four kids.

Deb   Four?! What did she do? Grow them in a greenhouse?

How did she find time to have four?

Jo   Well she was pregnant with her third when you last saw her and she's had another since then. Tone has a job down Co-op in Twerton I think. Lives Foxhill in Bath.

Do you remember Sam-Anne? Moved to fuckin' Jamaica and got herself two mixed-race kids and now speaks with some kind of weird Jamaican patois. All 'Jah bless' this and 'me do this' and 'me do that'. Stupid girl. Constantly on Facebook with her grievances bout boyfriends. Over sharin'. She's a waster.

Deb   Not your best friend then?

Jo   Never was.

Deb   So everyone's got their lives sorted then eh?

Jo   I don't think you could describe it like that no. I think you're the only one with a proper job.

Deb   What about you then? Don't want a career no more?

Year and a half ago you were goin' to be a vet.

Jo   With one A Level?

Deb   Alright but you were sayin' workin' down rescue centre and that.

Jo   Yeh well don't need to now, eh?

Deb   You doin' alright then?

Jo   Yeh.

Deb   Dad treatin' you alright then?

Jo   Yeh.

Pause.

Deb   Look sorry. But. Look. Do you know if. Dad's heard from Mum at all?

Jo   Don't think so. Maybe. I don't know half of what he's doing in that office.

Deb   Sorry.

Jo   No matter. You heard from her?

Deb   Only the once.

Jo   Listen, about it all.

Deb   Forget it.

Jo   It weren't very. I wasn't. I wanted to at least. Oh bloody hell.

A pause.

Deb   No matter.

A pause.

Deb   Do you know what the best thing out in the desert is?

Jo   What's that then?

Deb   A cold shower. Oh man that feels amazin'. End of the day. Not just because of the heat but gettin' all the dust and sand off you. Gettin' the sweat and the caked-on dust off your face. You could almost feel, doin' that, you could almost feel like you're treatin' yourself. Caring for yourself a bit. It was comfort. You know? Somethin' about water.

It makes everythin' new again. Clean. Untouched. You know? Oh shuttup Deb. Dickhead.

Jo   No don't. I know what you mean.

Deb   Yeh well.

Jo   It's like this weather. Aint it? We wait all this time for a fantastic summer and now all I want it to do is rain.

Deb   Yeh I guess.

A Pause.

Jo   When your letters would arrive I would take them to the garden to read them on my own.

A Pause. **Jo** *isn't looking at* **Deb**. **Deb** *isn't looking at* **Jo**.

Jo   I'm sorry. I don't know why I said that.

A pause. **Deb** *still can't bring herself to look at* **Jo**.

Jo   Sorry.

Jo *gets up and leaves.*

Scene Five

We transition again to the desert.

Sarko   Ah shit mate I'm done.

Deb   Why?

Sarko   Got another letter from Clare.

He hands her the letter and gets into his bunk as she reads it.

Deb   She's a real diamond aint she?

Sarko   I've got myself a class-A psycho there.

He grabs the letter and reads.

Sarko   '. . . last night I cried for three hours thinking about you.' or '. . . I can't help but wonder what the other girls there are like – are they fit?', '. . . whenever I touch myself I try to think of you and your cock but all I ever see is you blown to bits all over the desert.' It's like she wants me to get killed; it would fulfill her fucking fantasies or something.

Deb   She been out with soldiers before?

Sarko   Yeh.

Deb   Yeh.

Sarko *has some new lads mags and busies himself with ripping out pages with images of semi-naked women to put on the wall beside his bunk.*

Sarko   I got a mate who's on the subs – fuckin' easy life that. The girlfriends and wives have nothing to worry about as no women allowed on board. They lie about, reading and watching DVDs and can't call out so don't even have to speak to them. Fuckin' bliss mate. I'm in the wrong place.

Deb   Is Clare really that worried about you? You have told her I would rather have sex with a turd than go anywhere near you?

Sarko   Oh thanks mate, that's lovely. No. Anyway she thinks lesbians are fakin'. You've got boobs and a fanny. You're a threat.

Deb   Would it help if I spoke to her?

Sarko   Not in any way. She'll think it's some kind of cover up that we've orchestrated. No. I'm going to have to call it a day. Can't take the stress.

Deb   Fair enough.

Sarko   More hassle than they're worth.

Deb   Yeh.

Slight pause. **Deb** *gets some cards out and deals for them to play. Done wordlessly and as if done all the time.*

Sarko   You ever had a girlfriend then?

Deb   Nosy twat.

Sarko   I mean it. We've never spoken about it.

Deb   It's none of your business that's why.

Sarko   Why isn't it? You know about my birds.

Deb   Well that's because you've chosen to bore me rigid bout them.

Sarko   Oh sorry didn't realise it was borin'. Thought you were genuinely interested in my life.

Deb   I am. Just not all the fuckin' gory details alright?

Sarko   Why won't you tell me?

Deb   No one's business but mine.

They play on.

Sarko   Do you frig yourself off in your bed then? Or do you use the showers?

Deb   Fucksake! What is wrong with you?

Sarko   I aint had sex for four fuckin' months that's what's wrong with me!

Deb   Get control over yourself, seriously!

Sarko   Yeh but do you?

Deb   No!

Sarko   Not even a little bit?

Deb   What the fuck is a little bit?! Like I'm toying with myself.

Being a pussy-tease to myself?!

Sarko   You must do. Seriously. I know you're not a man but you must be feeling it. Do you do it in the shower?

Deb   I am going to zip myself up in my bed in a minute if you don't stop this line of conversation.

Sarko   Yeh but when you do will you then flick yourself to sleep?

Deb   Oh my god!

Sarko   Seriously give me something. Anything.

Deb   What so you can use it as wank ammo?

Sarko   What do you think of when you do it? Celebrities?

That bird in Operations? Men?

Deb   Why would I think of men?

Sarko   I don't know. Isn't it like your own version of the 'forbidden'? Like straight women who fantasise about other women? Or men that do the same about men.

Deb   Something you want to tell me, Sarko? Got some little secrets of your own have you?

Sarko   No. Shuttup. It was just an example.

Deb   Seems like maybe more than that to me. Tell me what you think about when your beatin' yourself off then. No, I bet I know – it's bondage stuff with figures of authority innit? It's you and the Major tied up in a dungeon and fucking each other free!

Sarko   Shuttup is it. I aint tellin' you what I fantasise about.

Deb   Then why should I tell you about mine?

Sarko   So you admit you have them?

Deb   Of course I do.

Sarko   I fuckin' knew it. And don't be tellin' me you've completely ruled out sex with a man.

Deb   You fuckin' wish. Is this your way of seducin' a woman?

No wonder you end up with such psychos.

Sarko   No I'm just sayin' I bet that it's just that you've yet to meet the right one.

Deb   Ah! You're lookin' to convert me. Cure me even. Nice.

Good work on the ignorance there mate.

Sarko   I don't believe people are black and white like that/

Deb   /well yeh they are/

Sarko   /not like that, you know what I mean. I think people are just sexual by nature. I don't think you could hand on your heart say that you would never be turned on by a man.

Deb   So with that reasoning you could potentially be turned on by one too then?

Sarko   No that's different.

Deb   What? Why?

Sarko   Because it is. Women need men. For reproduction. It's programmed into your brains. Men just need to do the do. They just need to impregnate. It's just sex to them.

Deb   Any hole's a goal?

Sarko   Exactly.

Deb   Including arseholes belongin' to men?

Sarko   No! Well yes! But not in my case fucksake. You're not listenin' . . .

Deb   I am and all I'm hearin' is some horny idiot tryin' to argue his way into my knickers.

Sarko   Don't flatter yourself. I only wanted some ammo like you said.

Deb   Well alright I'll give you some.

Sarko   Yeh?

Deb   Yeh, go on then. I will. Here's somethin' to think about when your bashin' your tiny little anaemic bishop.

She pauses for dramatic effect . . .!

Think about me with the Major, with me watching him skull fuckin' you til you cum all over his shoes.

Sarko   OK I ain't playin' no more.

Gets up to leave.

Deb   Oh you don't like it on the other foot do you? I gave you your ammo, what you complainin' about?

Sarko   You're sick you are.

Deb   I'm sick?

Sarko   Was only tryin' to instigate a conversation.

Deb   Oh hold up a minute mate – let me just get out my tiny violin.

Sarko   See this is what I'm talkin' about.

Deb   Shut up your whining and make me a brew.

She holds up her empty mug.

Sarko   Treat me like your own personal maid you do.

Deb   Go on then.

Sarko   Fuck you.

He grabs the mug and leaves.

Deb   And to you to!

She chuckles to herself alone.

Scene Six

Back in Chippenham, kitchen. **Jo** *is sitting on the countertop looking down at* **Deb** *who is clearing up the cards.*

Jo   If you're stayin' a little while then. Well, there's a new shopping centre opening up in town pretty soon. We could get you kitted out.

Deb   Yeh alright.

Jo   Bet you're used to just wearing uniform all the time.

Deb   I had a bag of clothes in my room; where'd they end up?

Jo   In the loft. Almost chucked them if I'm honest. Let's sort you out with new stuff yeh?

Deb   What you sayin'?

Jo   I'm sayin' if you wear that crap when we go into town you'll be walkin' ten steps behind me like my Muslim wife that's what I'm sayin'.

Deb   I quite like the thought of that.

Jo   Don't get no ideas.

Deb   You're smiling.

Jo   Course I am. Happy to see you.

Deb   Are you happy the rest of the time though?

Jo   Oh don't start. He's your dad. Have some faith.

Deb   Aren't you bothered?

Jo   Bothered with what?

Deb   With his work. What he does.

Jo   Oh bloody hell. It's just sex Deb.

Deb   But is it love?

Jo   Oh well that's deep. What exactly is love, mate? Other than two people needin' each other?

Pause.

Deb   Love to me feels like cold water on hot skin.

Pause.

Jo   My nan was with gramps for sixty-five years. Sixty-five? I mean. Surely. Things change.

Deb   I don't know.

Jo   There's got to be other stuff that keep you going.

Somewhere to live.

Deb   Spose.

Jo   Security.

Deb   Sounds like you've got it sussed.

Jo   This aint a bad place to end up.

Deb   You used to say in your letters that you were bored.

Jo   I am.

Deb   Don't you want something else then? Some kind of change?

Jo   I don't know. No. I don't think so. No.

A really long pause. **Deb** *is working herself up to say something.* **Jo** *is busying herself.*

Deb   When I came back after my first tour. And you were there. I really thought. That what we had. Ah fuck it. I'm shit at this. Fuck it. Just wanted you to know.

A pause.

Jo   Alright then. Good. Sorry. Anyways. I'm goin' to bed. You got everything you need?

Jo *gets up.*

Deb   Not really. Have you?

Jo *doesn't know what to say. She leaves* **Deb** *on her own.* **Deb** *turns the lights out. Blacks out the room as best she can with the curtains. She sits at the table and lights a cigarette. Somewhere in the distant past* **Sarko** *lights a cigarette and watches her.*

Scene Seven

Deb *is alone in the kitchen with none of the lights on. Above her noises of a television can be heard. The noises sound normal at first but we soon realise that it is porn that is being watched.* **Deb** *is listening to this. There are some thumps and then the sound of a bed creaking in rhythm. This goes on for a bit. It stops and there are footsteps, a pause and then the sound of a toilet flushing. A pause and then footsteps of someone coming down the stairs. It is* **Jim**. *He enters in his boxers and turns the lights on. He starts at the sight of* **Deb** *in the dark.*

Jim   If I didn't know better I'd think you had a death wish on me. Sittin' here in the dark you fuckin' vampire. What you doin'?

Deb   Sorry.

Jim   Why aintchoo in bed then?

Deb   Couldn't sleep.

Jim   You get that from me you do. I ant never been much of a sleeper. Used to stay up all night watchin' telly or readin' my comics.

Deb   Comics?

Jim   Yeh! All them superhero ones. Can't go wrong. I was just gettin' some water but I'll have a beer if you will.

Deb   Go on then.

Jim   Thas me girl.

Jim *gets them both a beer from the fridge.*

Deb   What about Jo?

Jim   She'll be asleep in less than five seconds I'll say. She could sleep through a tornado of pissing sharks she could. Lazy bitch.

Deb   Nice.

Jim   Don't mean it. So. No more desert. No more orders. You must be fuckin' relieved. Just glad you quit before you were blown to bits somewhere in the desert.

Deb   It was just a job to me. I can find another.

Jim   No need to look. Got one right here.

Deb   What? As what? Your chief porn supervisor? Your 'porn buyer'?! No thanks.

Jim   No. As something web based. You could pick up the ropes pretty quick I reckon. Design my sites. Do some administration for the company, that sort of thing. My second in command I suppose. Father and daughter. 'Jim and Daughter' we could call ourselves.

Deb Give me a break! A father and daughter team that specialise in porn. It sounds like a bad Channel Five documentary.

Jim It's a job. And I'm offerin' it to you.

Deb Yeh but it's got to be a job that I actually want to do.

Jim You sayin' you actually wanted to do the stuff you did out in Afghanistan?

Deb Sometimes.

Jim I still don't know where this comes from. You were always a tomboy but I never thought no daughter of mine would be a soldier that's all.

Deb I was also a peacekeeper.

Jim And you believe that do you?

Deb Yeh actually. The people out there are greatful to us.

Jim OK.

Deb We're providin' them with relief. When we have to shoot, then we're talkin' Taliban. The fuckin' evil ones. The bad guys. It's necessary.

Jim Alright. But what's the point in possessin' a womb if you're also a killer?

Deb WHAT?! Hold on a minute. Is this about? Is this about me or is this about; wait, what is it about?

Jim Just don't like it.

Deb What?

Jim Somethin' just doesn't quite sit with me.

Deb About what? Say it.

Jim You're a woman Deb.

Deb And there it is! I fuckin' knew it. You're a broken fuckin' record.

Jim   I just don't. It doesn't feel right. In my bones.

Deb   Your poor old bones – so sensitive to change. Will they ever adapt? No they fuckin' won't because they are sitting in the core of a man that thinks that the world is flat and all women are bitches.

Jim   Just talkin' about the facts mate. Men can't cope with it. If you're a bloke and a soldier goes down you have to keep goin'. But how you supposed to do that if it's a woman; cryin' and screamin' in pain? You can't leave her; and then your mission is fucked aint it? And come on mate – mixed barracks? Don't tell me you don't have trouble. You cannot say that on a six-month tour you aint gonna have people shaggin' around, it just aint natural. And it also aint professional. So put that in your pipe and fuckin' smoke it.

Deb   Hold up – male soldiers 'can't cope' with seein' us injured? 'Can't cope'? Oh fuck off. I'm sorry but if we're in a battle situation – which by the way I have been in; I have been shot at and I have shot back. Just because it aint the official line don't mean it don't happen. If we're in a battle situation and the bullets are flyin' round your head and you're runnin' for cover and you see your mate shot down. Regardless of their sex you will do what you can to get them out of harms way, assess their condition, call a medic and then continue on your way. Regardless. And any male soldier that becomes a jibberin' wreck at the sight of a bleedin' woman shouldn't have become a soldier in the first place. And do you know what? I was just as good if not better in that situation than my fellow male soldiers. Because I had to be. And I was carryin' 50 pound of kit in 50 degree heat. Can you do that you fat bastard? Course you can't 'cos you aint trained. But I am. And someone gave me that chance and I took it and I proved that I was capable.

Jim   Sounds like you're tryin' to convince yourself and not me.

Deb   Think what you like.

Jim   What about your periods then?

Deb   What?!

Jim   What do you do if you're in the middle of the battle and you get a period?

Deb   Suddenly I'm really tired.

Jo *appears in the doorway in her dressing gown.*

Jo   What's all this noise then?

Jim   Debs is on one of her feminist rants.

Jo   Good for her.

Jim   Oh don't you start an all. I'm completely fuckin' outnumbered now in-I? So on that note I'm goin' to go to bed. And I'll leave you two girls to discuss your monthly cycles.

Deb   Yeh yeh.

Jim   Night then.

Jim *leaves.* **Jo** *and* **Deb** *sit in the dark together. A short pause. Something passes between them.*

Deb   I don't know what I'm even talking about anymore. After everything that's gone on.

Jo   He been riling you up has he?

Deb   No.

Jo   We got our anniversary comin' up. Your dad's gonna take me to Wookey Hole.

Deb   He's what?

Jo   Shuttup I love that place!

Deb   So did I – when I was nine.

Jo   Shuttup.

Deb   You're a fuckin' mystery to me.

Jo   Well at least I'm something to someone eh?

Deb   What? You see? You say you're OK then you say shit like that. What am I supposed to think?

Jo   Sorry.

Deb   Why you sorry?

Jo   I don't know. This all just feels like a rubbish welcome home. Burnt bloody lasagna. That's what tonight was. It was a burnt lasagna.

Deb   It don't matter.

Jo   I know what'll make it better though.

Deb   What?

A pause. **Jo** *smiles at* **Deb**.

Deb   What?

Jo   You know what. Ready? OK then. Gold.

Deb   Oh come on.

Jo   Gold.

Deb   Idiot.

Jo   No, come on! Gold.

Deb   Fine! Leaf.

Jo   Tree.

Deb   Tops.

Jo   Bottom.

Deb   Cheeks.

Jo   Face.

Deb   Mask.

Jo   Hide.

Deb   Under.

Jo   Over.

Deb   End.

Jo   Finish.

Deb   Stop.

Jo   Start.

Deb   Begin.

Jo   Again.

Deb   Repeat.

Jo   Copy.

Deb   Cat.

Jo   Whiskers.

Deb   Beard.

Jo   Man

Deb   Woman

Jo   Beautiful

Deb   Hair

Jo   Brush

Deb   Clean

Jo   Tidy

Deb   Up

Jo   Down

Deb   There

Jo   Here

Deb   You

Jo   Me

Deb   I

Jo   Lids

Deb   Close

Jo   Shut

Deb   Lock

Jo   Tight

Deb   Fast

Jo   Slow

Deb   Dance

Jo   Move

Deb   Out

Jo   Reach

Deb   Grab

Jo   Take

Deb   Hold

Jo   Hug

Deb   Kiss

Jo   Touch

Deb   Caress

Jo   Kiss

Deb   No repetition!

Jo   Why not?

Deb   That's the rules.

Jo   Why do we need rules?

A pause.

Jo   Kiss.

A pause.

Jo   Kiss.

Scene Eight

Afghanistan. Day. The makeshift gym which is an outside affair.
Deb *and* **Sarko** *are lifting weights and spotting for each other.*
Sarko *is lifting at the start.*

Deb   Thing is that I heard from her just before when she said she was off to, I don't know, 'find herself' I guess. Greece she said. And now I aint heard from her since and I'm worried she's lost herself instead. And I know that these retreat things can mean she don't have no connection to the outside world, I mean that she won't be on email or nuffin'. And she don't even have a phone and that. And I know I'm being an idiot because I shouldn't expect anythin' else from her. But it was the first, only letter I ever got from her and it wasn't making much sense. And I got this feeling that. Well I thought I'd get more. Or a postcard from Greece or something. I don't know. She said some things about Dad and. I don't know.

Sarko *stops to catch his breath.*

Sarko   Maybe she's joined a cult.

Deb   Thought you were tryin' to make me feel better about this.

Sarko   Just from what you've said about her she sounds like a fuckin' lunatic.

Deb   If I said that about your mum you'd punch my fuckin' head off.

Sarko   Yeh but my mum's an angel. According to you, yours is a 'hippy slut'.

Deb   Fuck you dickhead.

Sarko   Just repeatin' what you said.

Deb   I can say it – she's my mum.

Sarko   Whatever.

Deb   Shuttup and finish your reps.

Deb *watches in silence as* **Sarko** *completes his set.*

Deb   What if it is a commune? Fuck.

Sarko   Look, she's just being a selfish cunt and not tellin' no one where she is. Pretty soon she'll get in touch and then you can have a go at her for being a bitch.

Deb   Yeh and the rest.

Sarko   Your turn. Reduce the weight?

Deb   Piss off.

Deb *gets into position and* **Sarko** *lowers the weight for her. It is heavy but she is able to do it.*

Sarko   You're gettin' better you know?

Deb *can't answer and completes her rep.* **Sarko** *helps her get the weight on the stand and she breathes heavily.*

Sarko   They can say what they like about you; but you can bench with the best of them.

Deb   Is that a compliment Sark? Fuckin' hell.

Sarko   Don't get used to it.

Deb   And what do you mean 'they can say what they like about me'? What do they say?

Sarko   You don't want to know.

Deb   Yeh I do. What do they say?

Sarko   Nothin'! It was a figure of speech you paranoid dick.

Deb   No it wasn't. I know they say shit. What do they say?

Sarko   Why do you care?

Deb   That's my fuckin' decision. Tell me.

Sarko   No. Do your second set.

Deb   No. Tell me.

Sarko   Do your fuckin' set, Deb.

Deb   No, fuckin' tell me.

Sarko   They don't say nothin'. I meant it. No one has a problem with you.

Deb   Now you're fuckin' lying.

Sarko   I'm not! You're being a stupid prick. Do your set.

Deb   Well they can all fuck off anyways. I've had enough of the shit I get. Fuck them.

Sarko   What shit? You don't get any shit.

Deb   Yeh I do.

Sarko   Shuttup.

Deb *concentrates and does her rep harder and faster than before. She grunts in pain. When she finishes she lets out a yell.*

Deb   Show me another fuckin' woman who can do that! Show me one other woman who can fuckin' do that!

Sarko   Easy mate, calm down. You're actin' like you got somethin' to prove.

Deb   Yeh well I have haven't I?

Sarko   Only to yourself.

Deb   Where's my mum, Sarko? Where's my fuckin' mum?

Sarko   What is this about? Lower your voice.

Deb   She's disappeared and my dad aint communicatin'. The only person that writes is Jo and she's. She's. I don't fuckin' know what she wants. And why am I here?

Sarko   It's your job you said. Best army in the world you said.

Deb   But why am I here? No one wants me here.

Sarko   Oh come on dickhead.

Deb   I'm serious. I put my life into this place.

Sarko   Get over yourself mate. You aint so special. We all feel like that.

Deb   Then what's the fuckin' point?

Sarko   I'm the fuckin' point. The lads are the fuckin' point.

We can all be each other's point. Whatever and that. Whatever. Shuttup. What's wrong with you?

Deb   I'm not cryin'.

Sarko   Yeh you are.

Deb   What the fuck is goin' on? Where is she?

Sarko   Pissin' about in the sunshine. What do you care? Thought you hated her? Thought she was a psycho?

Deb   Yeh.

Sarko   Anyways. This is home for us aint it?

Deb   This place is fuckin' scary, Sark.

Sarko   Of course it is.

Deb   You always look so together. You always look like you're in your element.

Sarko   So do you.

Deb   Do I? Don't feel it.

Sarko   You aint special, Deb. Everyone feels like that.

Deb   I just need somethin' that. I. Comfort. I'm fuckin' soft in- I? Fuckin' pussy that's what I am.

Before she can protest **Sarko** *kisses her. He holds her so she can't pull away and she struggles then lets it happen. When he stops and moves away she punches him in the face incredibly hard. He recoils holding his bleeding face.*

Deb   Prick!

Deb *is crying now. She can't stop herself.*

Deb   That's not what I meant. That's not what I fuckin' meant.

She runs off.

Scene Nine

Chippenham. The kitchen again with **Jo** *and* **Deb**.

Jo   It's so nice havin' you around again. I wish you felt like you could relax.

Deb   I'm just watchin' you and you don't seem the same no more. Sound stupid but you've almost changed shape.

Jo   Look. You're worryin'. Your dad's a lovely bloke.

Deb   No he aint.

Jo   He is. He looks after me.

Deb   Does he?

Jo   He provides for me.

Deb   Barely.

Jo   I don't know what you've dreamt up.

Deb   I know him is all.

Jo   And I know how to handle him.

A pause.

Deb   When I was out there I would have to search the women. On patrol. I would do this and I never once found anything other than what you'd expect. A body. Arms.

Legs. Breasts. Under all that fabric. It got me wonderin' about them as bodies. 'Cos they're so covered up but underneath. I mean. What kind of sex must they have with their husbands?

Jo   You're interested in everyone's business aren't you?

Deb   Like. I'm looking at this woman and thinkin' it must be pretty shit livin' under all that cloth all the time. I'm thinkin' her

husband must be keepin' her under lock and key. That their sex
must be horrible. But have I got it wrong? Is it actually really
fuckin' sensual? When they're home and behind the bedroom door.
Do you think she lets him undress her really slowly? Releasing her
hair, her face, her skin? Does he drink in every part of her before
kissing her all over? Knowing that he's the only one on this earth
who is doing that. Right there. In that moment. The two of them.
Or am I assumin' right? Is is cold, mechanical, brutal?

Jo   Well I guess you'll never know.

Deb   Sometimes what you see can be misleadin'.

Jo   Yes, what?

Deb   Tell me what I'm seeing is misleadin'.

Jo   He's your dad, Deb, why you bein' like this?

Deb   What's he like in bed?

Jo   Shuttup!

Deb   Is he gentle?

Jo   Stop it.

Deb   Kind? Lovin'? Generous?

Jo   Stop.

Deb   Does he make sure you cum first? Does he kiss you?

Does he get you ready before he goes in?

Jo   Deb . . .

Deb   Or does he just take it? Does he make you suck it? Does he
watch the nasty ass porn while he's fuckin' you from behind.

Jo   I don't mind though.

Deb   Really?

Jo   No. I don't. In fact. Sometimes I actually like it. Oh aint that a
shocker. 'Woman likes porn' I can see the headlines now. Gets me
goin' sometimes.

Deb   Alright then . . .

Jo   I find this bloody filthy woman inside me who wants to do all sorts of things, and I like it. It's that buzz. It's fun. It's a fantasy. It's somethin' to look forward to in my day when I get to let go and do as I'm told. Not everythin' is fairy lights and scented flippin' candles. I don't want a cuddle, I want to be fucked. Oh you don't like that do you? Suddenly regrettin' askin' are you? Sorry I aint perfect. Sorry I aint pure. And it's nothin' to be ashamed of anyways. I know what I like.

The distinction between Chippenham and Afghanistan gets blurred from here. **Sarko** *and* **Jim** *and* **Jo** *appear in both.*

Sarko   I wanted to talk to you. Why you been avoidin' me? I should be the one . . . punching me in the fuckin' face?

Deb *doesn't respond.*

Sarko   Look I am sorry. I am. Last thing I want to do is piss you off. Say something please.

Deb   It's OK.

Sarko   But it's not though is it? You're angry. Look. I guess. Look. I got carried away. I thought you wanted it because you and me, we're. Well we're different aint we? I can talk to you. I appreciate that. It makes sense you know? I like what we've got.

Deb   What have we got?

Sarko   Well you know. It's easy aint it? You let me talk, you understand me. And, you know, I protect ya.

Deb   You what?

Sarko   Keep an eye on things for ya. It's difficult out here and that. I don't mind. I don't mind lookin' after ya.

Deb   Is that what you think you're doing?

Sarko   Well yeh Deb. It's obvious aint it? How else would you have kept the other lads off your back? They know to stay away because you're with me. They know you're my girl.

A shift.

Deb   The thing is, I don't like it. I'm sorry I just don't. And I don't like you talkin' to me bout it alright? I have no interest in it. In fact I think it's horrible. And just because you think you're some kind of enlightened human bein' to be so liberal about it all don't mean that I have to.

Jim   It's just sex.

Deb   I'm sorry, you can justify it as much as you like but I don't like it. And I'm guessin' neither did Mum.

Jim   What's she got to do with it?

Deb   You tell me.

Jim   Look your mum had issues. She was messed up way before I got to her. We weren't right together. I know it's hard to hear but she wasn't a good person.

Deb   What is a good person then?

Jim   Well now. There's a question.

Another shift.

Sarko   Why you lookin' at me like that?

Deb   Where did you get all this from? We're mates. I aint your 'girl'.

Sarko   You know what I mean.

Deb   No I don't. I don't need nobody lookin' out for me.

Sarko   I thought I was doing you a favour. You're takin' this all wrong. I mean fair play you've done well out here but all I'm sayin' is that I've been on my guard. For you.

Deb   You're fuckin' delusional.

Sarko   Look whatever. You can't say that you haven't noticed. Us. Noticed. Things.

Deb   Who the hell do you think you are?

Sarko What?

Deb All my life I've been able to look after myself so why the fuck would I need you now? I can't believe you got me so wrong.

Sarko I'm sorry Deb but I don't think you're being honest with yourself.

Deb What? I've done nothing but work my arse off to prove myself to you fucking pricks and you still think I need protecting? I knew you were a stupid cunt but I didn't realise you were this bad. And by the way even if I was interested in men; why the fuck would I want you?

Another shift.

Jim Your mum would leave you in your room, lock the door and go down the pub. I don't know why you've got this obsession with her. She was a fuckin' awful mother. Don't you remember what it was like? She was a depressive. She was this massive cloud hangin' around. I tried everythin'.

Deb Like what?

Jim Well I dunno. She was hard to live with. You must remember. It weren't all me you know. You were just as bad with her.

Deb Yeh I know.

Jim I don't know why you're pinnin' so much on her. She's gone Deb. She's a waster. She's not worth it.

Pause.

Deb Why did she get so depressed?

Jim Well I don't fuckin' know do I? She was a nutjob, Deb!

Why does anyone go mad?

Deb She weren't mad. No she weren't. She was lost. I remember the arguments. I remember the bitchin'. The insults. I remember her bangin' around the kitchen in tears. I remember you in the telly room, smokin' and ignorin' her. I remember you just not sayin' anythin', walkin' past her in the hallway when she was slumped on the stairs, unable to move herself because she was so fuckin' sad. I learnt stuff from you, you know? I learnt that this was all normal. That when Mum was like this you just leave her be. Let her blow off steam. Let it pass. I ignored her like you. But really what we should have done. What you should have done, Dad. Was take her in your arms and hold onto her as tight as you could. That's what you should have done. So why didn't you?

Jim   When you came along it was like her light switched off for good.

Deb   What?

Jim   She may have had some kind of mad in her from the start mate, but as soon as you appeared; she'd gone.

A shift.

Jo   Look at your face. It's like I'm openin' up a whole new world for you. But don't get me wrong. I don't like the fake stuff. The professionals with their tits and no hair. It's all just so, I don't know, clean. And sex aint clean is it? It's filthy. It's sweaty and smelly and sticky. It's awkward. And uncomfortable. And sometimes a bit humiliatin'. And I like that. So when I'm watching I like it when it's more real.

Like, real people's sex. On 'youporn' or whatever. Real couples and that. We're lookin' in on them and seein' all the things they're up to. All the nasty, weird things. In their bedrooms, in their cars, in their kitchens. Their strange bodies, their noises, fumblings, twisting, fucking. And actually it's really quite hot. I like it.

Deb   So you'd do it would you? Put yourself up there?

Jo   Course I would. I have.

Deb   What?

Jo   Well, Jim did.

Deb   What are you talking about?

Jo   Jim put one up.

Deb   He did what?

Jo   He put it on. He put it. He put it online.

Deb   . . .

Jo   It's fine.

Deb   What is it of?

Jo   Of us. You know.

Deb   . . .

Jo   But it's OK. I don't mind

Deb   . . .

Jo   I don't. It's funny. It was night vision so my face looks like one of them zombie faces in a movie or somethin'. I didn't even know he was filming.

Deb   . . .

Jo   And my fat arse.

Deb   . . .

Jo   And it's not even that long. It's only about a minute or two. And it's not all that interestin'. Just my bum. And his. Can't see him actually. Just me. And my zombie face. All these thousands of people lookin' from god knows where around the world. At my bum. Those thousands of people.

Deb   . . .

Jo   Oh god.

Deb   . . .

Jo   But. It's OK anyways, because you wouldn't know it was me. You can't tell that it's me.

Deb   Is it still on there?

Jo   Yes. But he said he wouldn't do it again.

Deb   How do you know he won't?

Jo   Well I don't do I? I just have to trust him.

Deb   Why you pretendin' to me? Why you pretendin' everythin' is OK?

Jo   I'm not.

Deb   You are. It's fuckin' killin' me. Stop it. You're shakin'.

Jo   I can't

Jo *breaks down. A shift.*

Sarko   I got a theory about you.

Deb   Oh here we go . . .

Sarko   You keep everythin' so close to your chest. You hide as much as you can. But really I don't think that there's anythin' there. I don't think you're hidin' anythin'. It's all about the mystique. You create an air of mystery and people think you're more interestin' than you are. Just because you appear to have secrets don't mean your secrets are all that interestin'.

Deb   You're talkin' out of your fat arse.

Sarko   No I aint. I know a million women like you. You keep us guessin' because the truth is so mundane. All the prick teases down the pub makin' out like they're so fuckin' special. Only givin' over titbits of information. Suggestively lookin' at you when they've said somethin' that could mean somethin' else. It's all a fuckin' game to you lot aint it? It's all just about drivin' us mad with fuckin' lust and then expectin' us to just take a deep breath and walk away.

Deb   You've got a very high opinion of yourself haven't you?

Sarko   Fuck off do I. I'm just sayin' I think you're nothin' but hot air. And I don't believe a word of it; you've had girlfriends? Fuck off. You're so poppin' for it you couldn't be more obvious if you tried. You're kiddin' yourself, Deb.

I think you're all talk and actually. Actually you're a fuckin' lesbo virgin and what you really need is a damn good screw.

A shift.

Jim   What happens between a man and wife is their business.

Deb   Not when it's clear that what's goin' on aint makin' them happy no more. You proud of your work are you? You really proud of what you do?

Jim   Oh come on, Deb. You've seen it. You've seen how dark it is out there. I'm on the surface of it. Not even scratchin' it. I'm the tip of the flippin' iceberg what's gonna send us right down into the pits of hell/

Deb   /dramatic/

Jim   /There are people out there with things in their head that you don't even want to glimpse. The majority of people have thoughts every fuckin' day that, if they ever acted on them, you'd be yellin' for the return of capital fuckin' punishment. Don't you tell me you've never wanted to really hurt someone? Attack someone? Come on! Course you have! You're a soldier; you're programmed to think these things. But what if it don't stop there? Suddenly your punching someone. Choking someone. Cuttin' someone. It aint such a leap to the nastier stuff then. Is it? We like the base, the dirty, the wrong. We fuckin' lust after it every waking hour. So why, when we're all thinkin' it, can't we indulge in it? Just a bit? Just to relax? Not hurtin' no one. Just a man and his computer.

Deb   But it aint though is it? It aint. Sometimes it aint just a computer.

Jim   Well that aint my problem is it? All I'm sayin' is that we can't go against our nature. Why deny what we really are?

Deb   I think, Dad. That sometimes you think I'm your son. I think that sometimes you forget I'm a woman.

A shift.

Sarko   I reckon you're a virgin in both senses. Completely unexplored. Aint that true?

Deb   You better take that back. Who the fuck . . .?

Sarko   Just tryin' to instigate a debate darlin'. You like debates I thought. Why aint you playin' along?

A shift.

Jim   And when you're dealin' with psychos then there's no boundaries as far as I'm concerned. Your mother was a waster. She had no direction. She gave me shit most days. It wore me down. What's the point in havin' a wife if you can't have it on tap whenever you want it?

A shift.

Sarko   What's the point in havin' you out here if there's not goin' to be no perks?

A shift.

Deb   And I felt like I was floating somewhere between a massive bottomless pit and a huge gaping black hole. There was no light anywhere. Anywhere. No light at all. And do you know what I did? I shut my eyes and I thought of you.

A shift.

Sarko *uses his strength to overpower* **Deb**. *They struggle. He pushes her down facing away from him and holds her head on the floor with his hand. He pulls her trousers and knickers down and fucks her aggressively from behind.* **Deb** *doesn't make a sound.* **Jo** *and* **Jim** *watch impassively.* **Deb**'s *eyes are screwed up shut. When* **Sarko** *has finished he doesn't pull* **Deb**'s *trousers up but instead does his own trousers up and leaves.* **Jim** *leaves also.* **Deb**, *still seated, pulls her trousers up then moves slowly to the wall. Reaching up she hits a button and a shower is activated. She sits huddled as the water comes down and lets it soak her.*

Scene Ten

Jo   You were always quietly watchin' everythin'. Always on the edge of the group. Chucklin' at the jokes, never sayin' much though. Big sunny days by the river. Smokin'.

Drinkin'. Backies on the bikes. Huddled together round a
disposable BBQ trying to cook bacon. Swimmin' in our knickers
and t-shirts. And you. There on the sidelines watchin'. Not quite
confident enough to join in proper. But we didn't mind you 'cos
you would always bring crisps wouldn't you? And booze from
your dad's cupboard. And you'd always laugh at my jokes. You
were a kid I suppose but so were we. And you never really seemed
to mind that you were different. Your big green eyes. I remember
Craig noticed and would joke that he'd have to have a word with
you 'eyein' up his bird'.

Deb   I didn't know I was that obvious.

Jo   Pining.

Deb   Sorry.

Jo   Don't be. You know your letters you left for us? Ones we
weren't supposed to open unless.

Deb   You opened yours didn't you?

Jo   Yeh. Sorry.

Deb   Don't matter now anyway.

Jo   Thank you. For those things you wrote.

Deb   Don't matter.

Jo   Yeh it does. You promise you're not going back?

Deb   Yeh.

Jo   Good.

Deb   I don't have nothin' there no more. I thought it was my
family but it aint.

Jo   We're your family, Deb.

Deb   Not really.

Jo   I wish I was.

Deb   Come with me.

Jo   Where?

Deb   I don't know.

Jo   I can't.

Deb   She said I was to. Come with her. I was to find her. I was to. And I thought 'Fuck you'. I thought 'why would I do that?'. Fucking psycho. But. She. Isn't. She's this woman. Who is who I. Need. Jo. I. Oh. I need her. So badly. Oh god I don't know where she is. And she thinks I hate her. And I don't. Oh god I don't. And she's nowhere. And someone has ripped out everything inside me. I feel ripped clean. Ripped empty. And she can't want me. Why would she want me? She won't want me.

Jo   She was fightin' for you, you know?

Deb   What?

Jo   That night in the pub. When she heard about me and your dad. She came in when I was workin' and she dragged me off a stool. She went at me. And I didn't stop her. Because I knew she was right. But, Deb, she didn't come for me because of your dad. It was because of you. She was angry with me because I'd done this to you.

Deb   What?

Jo   I promise. It's completely the truth. She was fighting for you.

Deb   Come with me.

Jo   No.

Deb   Come with me.

Jo *leaves.* **Deb** *is alone.*

Deb   When you go out you get your kit and they take your photo. We call them the 'death photos' because they're the ones they will use to send to the press when you're injured or killed. In my last tour they took the photo and I was blinkin'. Fucksake. They were in a rush so they wouldn't let me do another and they were all like 'better make doubly sure you don't get killed then hadn't you?'. It really fucked me off. Because I knew that if I did then I would definitely have my stupid blinkin' photo in every bloody newspaper and then that would be it. That would be the only way people remember me. Because even if there has been multiple deaths you will always get a photo of the female soldier because that's interestin' to folk. That's what sells papers aint it?

Anyway. So yeh. They take your photos. But before that what you do is write your letters. To be opened by your loved ones in the event of your death. Man that was hard. Writin' them. What do you say? With dad's I just basically said a load of mundane shit about lovin' him and 'despite the ups and downs' etcetera. With Jo I told her how I felt and what a wonderful woman I think she is. But with Mum.

Well for a start it was all a bit bloody academic because we didn't have an address for her so actually I still got the letter with me. But I wanted to still write it. And I said.

Well.

She gets the letter out and reads.

OK. All the usual stuff about missin' her and that. That I love her no matter what. But.

She reads for a moment.

What I didn't write. And what I should have. Was. That I think that she has this, like, massive huge heart inside her and that no one's let her use it properly. And that I'm sorry for not. For not standin' up for her more.

She puts the letter back in her pocket.

I've been covered in this thin film of dust see? Not just in the desert. I've felt like my skin hasn't been able to breathe.

Deb *holds her face up to the sun, breathes in and smiles. Lights fade to black.*

End.

The Wasp

Morgan Lloyd Malcolm

The Wasp was first performed at Hampstead Theatre Downstairs, London on 29 January 2015 with the following cast:

Heather   Sinead Matthews
Carla   MyAnna Buring

Creative Team

Writer: Morgan Lloyd Malcolm
Director: Tom Attenborough
Production Manager: Andy Reader
Designer: David Woodhead
Lighting Designer: Joshua Carr
Sound Designer: Fergus O'Hare
Assistant Director: Abigail Pickard Price
Stage Manager: Philippa Sutcliffe
Composer: Edmund Rex
Movement Director: Scott Ambler
Fight Director: Bret Yount

Original Production

The original Hampstead Theatre production of *The Wasp* transferred to Trafalgar Studios 2, London, opening on 8 December 2015, produced by Tim Johanson and Mark Cartwright.

Heather   Laura Donnelly
Carla   MyAnna Buring

Creative Team

Writer: Morgan Lloyd Malcolm
Director: Tom Attenborough
Designer: David Woodhead
Lighting Designer: Oliver Fenwick

Sound Designer: Luke Swaffield
Assistant Director: Amy Wicks
Production Manager: Ben Hosford
Stage Manager: Philippa Sutcliffe
Composer: Edmund Rex
Movement Director: Scott Ambler
Fight Director: Bret Yount

At the end of Act One and Act Two I have written for there to be blackouts. This is one version of how you can end them however in the original production Tom the director instead used the transitions to show the scene changes as they happen.

Without revealing too much of the plot in my description he had the actors move scenery and set up for the next act in full view of the audience and therefore no blackouts were used until the end of Act Three. I only mention this to free up future productions to be creative with how they move between acts.

The signal to 'blackout' is more of an indication of a definite end to the act – how you move to the next act is up to you and should be done in as efficient way as possible. There is nothing worse than a long blackout which the audience must sit through as they wait for the set to change . . .

Act One

A cafe. The outside smoking courtyard. **Carla** *sits with an ashtray full of cigarettes in front of her. She is pregnant. She is considering having another fag. She is in her early thirties though is dressed like she always has since her teens. Tracksuit bottoms, air-tex-shirt, necklace, slicked back hair. She fiddles nervously with her phone. She has a second phone that she also removes and looks at then puts away. One is a smart phone, one is a cheaper older phone.*

Heather *emerges from the entrance into the cafe. She is also in her early thirties but dressed up to date. Neat, simple, more expensive than high street. Statement handbag.*

Heather   Carla?

Carla   Yeh.

Heather   I'm so sorry! I didn't realise there was this bit out here. I've been in there all this time.

Carla   . . .

Heather   I texted you.

Carla   Yeh.

Heather   Did you get it?

Carla   I was just finishing my fag.

Heather   Course. Yes. Thought I'd just nip to the loo and saw this door. Glad I spotted you! Could have been sitting there ages. Both of us thinking the other was late.

Carla   I got here early.

Heather   Did you?

Carla   Yeh.

Heather   Do you want to come inside or . . .

Carla *lights a cigarette.*

Heather   Yeah, yeah . . . we can sit out here. I'll just rescue my latte.

Heather *goes and returns with her cup.*

Heather   Actually do you want a drink? I may get another.

Carla   Tea thanks. **Heather**: Milk and sugar? **Carla**: Yeh.

Heather   Right then.

Heather *leaves and* **Carla** *smokes and texts.* **Heather** *returns with two teas, a milk jug and some sugar sachets. Over the following* **Carla** *puts milk and four sugars into her tea.*

Heather   Thought I'd join you in a tea. Already had my coffee hit. Don't want to be bouncing off the walls! Got you a builder's. That right? Got myself a camomile. Trying to be good. Well, trying. Look at us!

Carla   Alright then are you?

Heather   Well how long? I mean. You haven't changed a bit.

Well. Other than. When are you due?

Carla   Couple of months.

Heather   Wow.

Carla   Thanks. You have.

Heather   Sorry?

Carla   Changed.

Heather   God I hope so!

Carla   What happened to the plaits. And the glasses then?

Heather   Oh long gone! Long gone! As soon as I went to uni I wised up and basically realised I had spent years looking like a complete idiot. No wonder. Well. No wonder you lot found it so funny.

Carla   Yeh well. Sorry about that.

Heather   Oh no bother. Water under the bridge.

We were all young.

Carla   I'm not like that no more.

Heather   Course.

Carla   I'm not. Problem with school is that you think that's everything and then you leave and you realise it's basically nothing and then you're like out in the world and you have to work with people and they didn't know you at school and like don't care and that.

Heather   . . .

Carla   That's why I was OK to meet you.

Heather   Right.

Carla   When you got in touch I thought, none of that old stuff matters no more. Course I can meet you.

Heather   I'm glad.

Carla   Cos if it were, like, almost twenty years ago then there's no way in hell I'd be seen dead with you right?

Heather   No.

Carla   But I reckon twenty years can make you wiser yeh?

Heather   Yes. Absolutely.

Carla   And I done stuff. So. And I can deal with this.

Heather   Great.

Carla   So. What do you want then?

Heather   Well. How are you? What have you been doing since we last saw each other? I mean I see the bits and bobs on socials but, well, you have kids now don't you?

Carla   Yeh. Four.

Heather   Gosh!

Carla   Had one straight after school, then another, then another, then another.

Heather   Yes.

Carla   Oldest is sixteen, youngest is six. And this one will make five.

Heather   Congratulations. CARLA: Thanks. They're alright.

Heather   Good.

Carla   Pretty hard work if I'm honest but I love them and that. What about you? You got kids.

Heather   Well, no. No. But I'd like to.

Carla   Better hurry up.

Heather   Yes I know.

Carla   I tell you what I'm glad I had most of mine when I was young and had energy and that. At least now I know what I'm letting myself in for. I can prepare.

Heather   Well, I guess I didn't really feel ready, I suppose.

Carla   Are you ever ready, that's what I say.

Heather   No. I guess not.

Carla   My old man wanted another and I just told him to fuck off.

Heather   So. What happened?

Carla   Just happened I guess. And now he's all happy about it.

Heather   And you're not?

Carla   Well he won't be the one getting up with it at night and changing nappies and such. He never helped with all that. He's traditional like that I think. Don't mind. But I do mind. You know?

Heather   Sometimes you need a second pair of hands I guess.

Carla   Yeh. He's alright I suppose but he's a lazy fat fuck too. And he's really old.

Heather   Really?

Carla   Yeh. In his sixties now. He'll probably die before this one's out of school.

Heather   Well I don't know, sixty is still young.

Carla   Not when you smoke forty a day and live off shit.

Heather   No.

Carla   It's alright I don't mind. And I have a plan anyways so . . .

Heather   Well I must say you seem pretty together for a mum of nearly five.

Carla   I have to be don't I?

Heather   And where do you work now?

Carla   Morrisons.

Heather   Oh yes?

Carla   Whatever. It's fine. Look, why did you want to meet?

Heather   Sorry. Yes. Look. I know that we weren't exactly mates at school, at least we were; when I first moved here, in fact you were my first, my only. My accent used to make you . . . anyway. After that. Before we got to that stage where you were with Kerry and that lot, and I very definitely wasn't? Do you remember before, in like year seven. When we would hang out after school?

Carla   Yeh. Sort of.

Heather   Do you remember that one day after school with the pigeon?

Carla   No.

Heather   Look it doesn't matter what happened. I just. It just made me think of you and I just realised I needed to speak to you. About something. Perhaps I should start at the beginning.

Carla   Yeh that would help.

Heather   Sorry.

Carla   Hold up.

She lights another cigarette.

Carla   Go on.

Heather   Sorry if this is all a bit too much information. I appreciate we haven't been in touch for years. I do appreciate that. But . . .

Carla   Get on with it.

Heather   Right so. My husband and I have been trying to conceive a baby for about four years now . . .

Carla   Ain't sex working?

Heather   Well, no . . .

Carla   Is it him? It's usually the man.

Heather   No, we've looked into it and it appears to be me, but . . .

Carla   You do know that there is only about two days when you are really ready yeh?

Heather   Yes we've done all the timings, we've tried everything I promise you. We've also tried some IVF but it's not working.

Carla   Gutting.

Heather   Yes. And so we're kind of just, I suppose, not giving up per se but, just taking it easy for a bit, not thinking about it. I've become a bit obsessed.

Carla   I got pregnant first time every time we tried.

Heather   Yes some people have that luck.

Carla   I wouldn't call it lucky. He only has to look at me and I'm pregnant. Do you think I wanted five kids?

Heather   Well I don't know but that's wonderful you have found it so easy.

Carla   Too easy.

Heather   Yes. Well we haven't.

Carla   There are things you can do . . .

Heather   Like I said we've tried them all.

Carla   You tried standing on your head after?

That's supposed to work.

Heather   We've tried everything.

Carla   Don't swallow yeh? No matter what he says that won't help neither.

Heather   No.

Carla   So what am I supposed to be able to help with?

Heather   So we've been trying four years and . . .

Carla   Do you want this one?

Heather   No no.

Carla   I'm only half joking mind. Or actually, I could carry one for you. I saw something about that surrogacy on telly and I was considering it you know?

Heather   Were you?

Carla   Yeh. Easy money. I don't mind being pregnant. But then I realised they'd probably want me to give up smoking even though it did no harm to my other four and I thought 'fuck that'.

Heather   Yes, smoking is probably one of those deal breakers.

Carla   So I would say that I'd have a baby for you if that helps but I'm not going to.

Heather   Well thank you for the thought.

Carla   How much would you pay me though?

Heather   Um.

Carla   Out of interest.

Heather   Look I promise I hadn't come here for that at all.

Carla   Yeh but how much?

Heather   I don't know what the norm is.

Carla   I think it's up to how much the couple are worth or something. You look like you're doing alright these days. How much would it be worth to you?

Heather   Well really it's priceless.

Carla   Yeh yeh, how much?

Heather   Look I wasn't here for that.

Carla   Couple of thousand? Couple of tens of thousands?

I'd do it for that. I'd give up smoking for that.

Heather   I'm sure you would. But look . . .

Carla   I'll do it.

Heather   What?

Carla   I'll do it. I'll have a baby for you.

Heather   Would you really do that for someone?

Carla   Yes. I need the money. I'm good at being pregnant. It's easy. Once I'm done with this one we can get on it.

Heather   . . .

Carla   Would you need one of my eggs too?

Heather   . . .

Carla   My eggs are obviously pretty good.

Heather   I really didn't come here for this.

Carla   But you're thinking about it aren't you?

Heather   . . .

Carla   Look. I know how it is. My mate Becs couldn't get pregnant and she was properly depressed about it. Took her years. They adopted in the end but she's still not OK about it. She wanted to have one of her own. And I know how just the once you want to experience the pregnancy thing but think about it this way; what if for you it's shit? Lots of people have shit pregnancies. At least if I do it for you it's still exciting and that but it's also no bother for you.

Heather   Look it's very kind . . .

Carla   I wouldn't mind. It would mean I could quit my job.

Heather   Thank you but I really don't want you to have a baby for me.

Carla   Why not?

Heather   It's not something I was considering.

Carla   I'd stop smoking.

Heather   It's not that.

Carla   Is it because of the kids? They would help.

Heather   No it's not that. Honestly, please. I don't want you to have a baby for me because I don't want one. Not with Simon.

Carla   Simon your husband?

Heather   Yes.

Carla   Who do you want one with then?

Heather   No one. I don't want one anymore. Well I do. But not with someone who. Look that's just it. I wanted to tell you something.

Carla   Go on.

Heather   This is in deepest confidence. Please don't tell anyone.

Carla   Go on.

Heather   He's been emailing another woman.

Carla   Hold up. I ain't very good at agony aunt shit. Just so you know. I ain't going to be much help so if that's why you wanted to meet.

Heather   No it isn't.

Carla   I'm not one for being nice in that . . . what's that word . . . understanding?

Heather   Empathising?

Carla   Whatever. I'm not good at that.

Heather   Please?

Carla   Go on.

Heather   He's been emailing another woman. It started about two years ago. When we were in a bit of a tricky patch. We'd already been trying for a couple of years and I wasn't taking it very well. We were only doing 'it' at the right times and it was putting a lot of pressure on. We weren't happy. No. We weren't happy at all really. So I can kind of understand. No I can't . . . But I can. Anyway. He started emailing this woman two years ago. Just flirty chats. Silly stuff. And nothing too bad. Until we had a particularly bad month and suddenly he started telling her things about us. About me. About my fertility problems. About how he wasn't finding me attractive any more. Horrible things.

Carla   Heavy.

Heather   And it carried on. It became sexy emails. Telling her what he wanted to do to her. Telling her that while he was having sex with me, he was thinking of her. That I wasn't sexy in any way. That I didn't turn him on anymore and so he had to imagine her so he could do what he needed to do. And the thing is that this has been going on now for two years and recently it stepped up a gear.

Carla   Sorry, hang on, go back a bit; two years? You've let this carry on two years?

Heather   I really wanted a baby.

Carla   With him?

Heather   Yes.

Carla   Go on.

Heather   So in the last week he's emailed her to say that he wants them to finally meet.

Carla   But how do you know?

Heather   The emails.

Carla   Exactly.

Heather   Sorry?

Carla   I'm sorry but I don't think you have much of a leg to stand on. You've been reading his emails for two years. You should have said something at the start. He's going to use that against you.

Heather   I haven't been reading them.

Carla   What?

Heather   Well I have but not in the way you think. I've not been accessing his account.

Carla   Then how do you know what he's been writing to her?

Heather   It's me.

Carla   Who's you?

Heather   The other woman. It's me.

Carla   . . .

Heather   He's been emailing me.

Carla   You crafty little cunt!

Heather   Well..

Carla   I love it!

Heather   I was paranoid he was cheating on me so a couple of years back I made a fake Facebook profile and messaged him. I was right to be paranoid though because he messaged back.

Carla   Yes he bloody did!

Heather   And I probably shouldn't have let it go on so long but he kept getting in touch.

Carla   You dark horsey cunt!

Heather   Yes alright.

Carla   I love it!

Heather   I'm not very proud of myself.

Carla   Why not? I would be!

Heather   Like you said, I don't really have a leg to stand on.

Carla   Oh fuck that. Honeytrap mate. You set a honeytrap and he went for it. Everyone does it.

Heather   Everyone?

Carla   Yeh! The only way to make sure your bloke isn't playing the field. I'm telling you. This is nothing. You remember Jolene?

Heather   Yes. Got expelled didn't she? The fire/

Carla   The fire in the gym. Yeh. Anyway. She lives Bristol way now and I see her time to time. Last I saw her she was in the middle of something like this. Her bloke is a bouncer, working most nights, and you know what bouncers are like. Getting chatted up by girls wanting to skip the queue. Being promised stuff in return for drink vouchers that kind of shit. She knew the game because that's how they met.

Heather   Right.

Carla   He'd let her and her mates in afterhours in return for a blow job or summat so she knew he was up for it. And obviously, you meet a bloke that way you're always gonna wonder.

Heather   Yes you are.

Carla   So she decided to see whether he would. She sent a friend down to the club one night telling her to try it on with him and he went for it. Not even a second to pause and think about it. Offered it on a plate, 'yes please, yumyumyum'.

Heather   What did Jolene do?

Carla   Screamed at him about it. Got him to promise never to do it again. Got pregnant.

Heather   She took him back?

Carla   Yeh. Hey maybe that could be how you get pregnant?

Have an argument?

Heather   Tried it.

Carla   Well look, all I'm saying is that this happens.

Men are like this see? And you have to catch them out

Heather   I didn't think he was like that.

Carla   Well course he is. I ain't never come across a man who isn't.

Heather   But not him.

Carla   They're all the same.

Heather   But that's not true. They aren't all like that.

Carla   They are.

Heather   No. Not in the world I live in. They don't all just chase after women or say yes to the first girl to offer a blow job or beat their wives or not change nappies.

Carla   Who said anything about beating wives?

Heather   You know what I mean.

Carla   No I don't.

Heather   It's disrespect. It's cruelty. It's violence actually. A level of violence. That is acceptable to some and not to others. It's basically normal. For them.

Carla   No it ain't to me. My bloke lays one finger on me or the kids and he's out. What are you going on about?

Heather I just think it's so sad you think that all men are capable of an affair.

Carla Don't blame me, blame their biology.

Heather No I disagree. It's nurture too. If they've been taught to respect their partner . . .

Carla Oh fucksake.

Heather No listen; if their parents have taught them the right way to behave.

Carla Yeh?

Heather Then they can resist biology. Surely. In my world people respect women.

Carla What's this world you keep going on about?

Is it different to mine?

Heather Yes it seems so.

Carla Why?

Heather You accept that this can happen. You accept it.

Carla Look you're the one with the husband looking elsewhere.

Heather Yes.

Carla So that makes you different to me how?

Heather I'm just saying/

Carla Just saying what? Cos so far all you've done is made me go out my way to meet you, chatted shit about your stupid husband and then basically insulted me and my friends.

Heather No please . . .

Carla Actually I'm just going to go.

Carla *gets up to leave.*

Heather No please don't. Don't. I'm sorry. I'm just very upset about what's going on and I'm not thinking about what I'm saying. I'm not thinking.

Carla   No you're not. I'm trying to give you good advice here. That was what you wanted wasn't it? And I told you I was no good at giving advice.

Heather   No it wasn't what I wanted.

Carla   So why the bloody hell am I here?! What the fuck?

I'm going.

Carla *starts to leave.*

Heather   No wait. The pigeon.

Carla   What?

Heather   The pigeon. In the fields out the back of the school. Do you remember? Me and you. On our way back home. That pigeon. With the broken wing.

Carla   What's the pigeon got to do with your husband?

Heather   You didn't just break its neck. End its misery. Did you? Nope. You wanted to pluck it first. Snap its feet off. Use a stone to crush its beak. Take its eyes out with a stick. Then you started stamping on it. Until it was all over the path. Blood, feathers, its insides. You could have done it quickly.

Carla   I'm going.

Carla *goes to walk out again.*

Heather   I want you to kill Simon.

Carla   What?

Heather   Kill him.

Carla   . . .?

Heather   I've got ten thousand pounds in this bag.

Carla   . . .

Heather   And there's another twenty once it's done.

Heather *waits for* **Carla** *to respond.*

Carla   What?

Heather   I think I've made myself pretty clear.

Carla   I . . .

Heather   He's lied, he's hurt, he's emotionally abused me.

I've had enough. I don't just want him out of my life I want him gone. Completely. And you're the only person I know who can do it. Kill him. Kill Simon. I want him dead.

They breathe.

Heather   You've done it before.

Carla   To a fucking pigeon! A pigeon! Are you mental?

Heather *just stares at her.*

Carla   What's wrong with you?

Heather   Thirty grand.

Carla   . . .

Heather   You're thinking about it aren't you?

Carla   No. Look. I don't know who you think I am but I'm not that. OK? You've made a mistake about this. I'm going.

Heather   It's a shit load of money.

Carla   Well not really actually. Not really.

Heather   Oh come now. It is when you have nothing.

Carla   Well that would be none of your business.

Heather   He's been gambling again hasn't he?

Carla   What?

Heather   Your bloke. What was it you said? 'That stupid cunt has lost our rent money again'.

Carla   . . .

Heather   You should be a bit more careful who you befriend on Facebook yourself.

Carla   You?

Heather   He's pretty fit though isn't he? I was proud of him. And good with words. I must say Carla – you have a filthy mind.

Carla *is completely silent. She almost looks like she could cry.*

Heather   I'm sorry. I know you were hoping he could be your ticket out of this place. But that's why I'm here. Thirty grand would help wouldn't it?

Carla   You invented a whole profile just to chat dirty shit to me?

Heather   I just needed to find out a bit more about you.

Before I made this proposition. You could be loaded for all I knew. I had make sure my offer wouldn't be rejected.

Carla   Well it will be. I can't do it.

Heather   Yeh you can.

Carla   I'm not like that.

Heather   Yeh you are.

Carla   Why do you want him dead? Why don't you just humiliate him or something? Put his emails on the internet? Why kill him?

Heather   It's not just his emails.

Carla   What is it then?

Heather   Not your problem.

Carla   Yes it is.

Heather   No it isn't. Look at you pretending. As if thirty grand isn't something you're desperate for.

Heather *pushes the bag closer towards* **Carla**.

Carla   You're joking aren't you? This is a joke. Are there people watching? Is this a TV show?

Heather   No.

Carla   You're mad then.

Heather   Not really.

Carla   I don't know who you think I am . . .

Heather   You're scrabbling. In the dirt. You're nothing. You've spent your life thinking something will happen to make things better but it hasn't. I think you even said online you'd do anything to get out of here. For your kids. You clearly love them. It's touching how much you actually wanted to chat about them. Thirty grand could relocate you all. Without the useless husband. Move to a different city. Rent somewhere nice. Start again. You need this.

Carla   No I don't.

Heather   Yes you do.

Carla   You've got me wrong.

Heather   . . .

Carla   You're wrong. Fuck you. You're wrong.

Carla *leaves.* **Heather** *waits. Suddenly* **Carla** *returns and* **Heather** *looks up at her.*

Carla   Thirty grand?

Heather   Yep.

Blackout.

Act Two

Heather's house. The front room. Nicely decorated. Modern.
Clean. Neat. On the wall are some collections of dead insects
behind glass. Mostly butterflies but there are some spiders and in
particular a Tarantula Hawk Wasp collection which has its own
display. **Heather** *has laid out some tea and biscuits on a coffee*
table and is busy plumping pillows when the doorbell goes. She
goes to answer it.

Heather (*offstage*)   Shoes off if you don't mind.

Carla (*offstage*)   Yeh.

Heather *leads the way into the sitting room and indicates for*
Carla *to take a seat.*

Heather   I'll be mother.

She pours the tea and offers a biscuit to **Carla**. **Heather** *watches*
as **Carla** *sips her tea.*

Heather   So. Here we are.

Carla   Yeh.

Heather   I'm glad you came.

Carla   Nearly didn't.

Heather   Well we both know that really that's not true.

Carla   Look just because I need the money doesn't mean I'll do
just anything. I've got some things I need to say.

Heather   Fire away.

Carla   Right . . .

Heather   It's important we do this properly. In fact let's treat this as a straight up business proposal. We are having a meeting. Shall I take minutes?

Carla   What? No! Fuck no.

Heather   It doesn't need to be obvious what we are talking about. It can just be to get something down in writing.

Carla   No! That's one of the things. We need a proper plan.

Thirty grand ain't worth the jail sentence for murder.

So whatever we decide it has to be fucking perfect. The perfect fucking killing. No paper trails. No nothing. Wait . . .

She indicates to **Heather** *as if to say 'is he here?'*

Heather   No, no. Of course not. He's out at one of his meets. I think it's rowing tonight. Or possibly salsa. I've stopped asking.

Carla   I should have checked before I started talking.

Heather   I wouldn't have let you talk don't worry. He won't be back for several hours.

Carla   Yeh. So what I was saying is that I ain't never done this before. Not a human anyways, so we want to work it out properly. No amateur shit. We don't want the police laughing at the evidence and saying, I don't know, like 'who are these fucking idiots who don't know how to cover their own tracks' and that.

Heather   You're absolutely right. We do it properly. CARLA: Which means it won't be happening quickly.

Heather   OK.

Carla   It means I want to scope out your place. Work out timings. Make sure nothing can go wrong.

Heather   You really do sound like you've done this before.

Carla   I've watched a lot of telly. I googled it. Since we met I've been researching. Carefully mind; not on my home computer, don't

have one, went down the library didn't I? So I know all the
common mistakes people make. I ain't planning to make them.

Heather   Like what?

Carla   Like fingerprints. Wearing gloves ain't I?

Holds up her gloved hands.

Heather   Oh very good.

Carla   And we're drinking tea but I'm reckoning you have a
dishwasher. I want you to make sure it's the hottest wash you got
when you clean it OK?

Heather   Of course.

Carla   And I ain't gonna let myself be seen when I come here –
that's why I came in the back. And when we do it we'll do it at
night. Cover my face. Make sure I have an alibi too. I don't know,
if it is night time then my husband will say I'm in bed with him
which wouldn't be lying for him because that's what he'll think.
He sleeps so heavy he wouldn't notice either way.

Heather   Right OK.

Carla   And when I do it I'll make sure the weapon is one I've got
from somewhere random and unconnected and I'll chuck it in with
the recycling at the dump.

Heather   Great.

Carla   So I was thinking we make it look like a botched burglary.
I've done a few house jobs before and I can do all the stuff needed
to make it look like I had broken in to steal. I'll take some stuff.
We'll call it collateral damage. It'll look more authentic that way.

Heather   Or I could make up some stuff so that you don't
actually physically have to take anything.

Carla   No I want to take some things.

Heather   What if you're caught with them?

Carla   I won't be. I will sell them on. Don't worry about that.

Heather   I'd really rather not lose any belongings.

Carla   What?

Heather   I mean. I'm already paying you an awful lot.

I'd rather we found an alternative.

Carla   You want me to kill your husband and you're worrying about losing your DVD player and some bits of jewelry?

Heather   Well if we could agree some not so important items.

Carla   You can lay out the things you don't mind going.

I can't believe we're talking about it.

Heather   I'm just not entirely convinced this is the best idea.

Don't you think it's a bit of a cliche?

Carla   A what?

Heather   I mean. A botched burglary. It's a bit *Midsomer Murders*. Wouldn't they see through it?

Carla   Well you come up with something then.

Heather   Actually I have.

Carla   Go on.

Heather   I cook him a lovely meal and slip something in his drink that sedates him. Once he's out I call you and that's when you kill him.

Carla   And then what?

Heather   Well you get rid of him.

Carla   What, like dispose of him? In bags? Where? Where would we do that?

Heather   Cut him up and put him in bags in the freezer then slowly . . . I don't know . . . feed him to a dog or something. Do you have a dog? Free dog food.

Carla   Jesus.

Heather   I mean it. If it's eaten it can't be discovered.

Carla   Fuck.

Heather   What?

Carla   You're fucked.

Heather   I'm just trying to be thorough. If you do a botched burglary you could leave evidence. This way we could get rid of it all.

Carla   So you can knock him out and cut up his body but you can't do the killing yourself?

Heather   Look there's a difference between slipping a bit of a sedative into someone's drink and hacking them to death. And I wouldn't be doing the disposing, that's your job, that's why I'm paying you.

Carla   And how do you explain his disappearance?

Heather   His infidelity. He's 'run away'. I assume he's left the country. I'm a scorned woman. Betrayed. He's the bad guy.

Carla   And when he never turns up? At all? Don't you think they would get suspicious?

Heather   I mean I don't know! I'll burn his passport or something. Make out like he's packed a bag. That he's properly gone. I don't know.

Carla   It's all a bit far-fetched. And to be honest it's violent.

For someone who/

Heather   /Oh and beating him up isn't violent?

Carla   Not saying it isn't. I'm just. You know. I mean you were the one going on about not being that kind of person. And here you are coming up with the worst kind of nasty shit.

Heather   That's why I need you. I can't do any of this myself.

Carla   Look are you sure you want him actually dead?

Heather   Yes.

Carla   Not just exposed and chased off in some way?

Heather   No.

Carla   Properly, brutally, murdered, dead.

Heather   Yes.

Carla   OK. Well if it's to be me and not you to do it then I want to do it my way.

Heather   I just think it's risky. What if he defends himself?

What if he overpowers you?

Carla   Nah you're right about that. So, OK, here's what we'll do then – some of your plan too. You drug him at dinner. Or better yet get him good and drunk. Pass out drunk.

Would that be possible?

Heather   Definitely.

Carla   And once he's out for the count you call me. I come over. Do it. Take some shit. And this time it'll look like a burglary that went wrong because he was drunk and trying to play hero. You need to take a sleeping pill or two and wake up in the morning to discover him, phone the police and report this horrible tragic crime. You went to bed after dinner leaving him having a night cap downstairs watching the telly, next thing you know it's morning and he's not in bed with you. 'Oh officer, whoever came knew exactly what they were doing – let themselves in the back door, helped themselves to my silverware but they didn't reckon on my husband being up and had to deal with it there and then. I'm so proud of him – defending me. I feel so lucky they didn't come upstairs!' Yeh? How does that sound?

Heather   Good.

Carla   Only good? I think it sounds fucking mint.

Heather   I'm just still a bit loathe to let go of too many of my belongings. Particularly my silverware.

Carla   Oh man you've got to let that go.

Heather   I may be getting rid of this man but I'm doing everything I can to make sure every other part of my life remains unaffected.

Carla   I'm not sure I can guarantee that. Things will change.

You're going to have to get your story straight.

Heather   I will.

Carla   No I mean really straight. They're going to question you. A lot. It won't be easy.

Heather   I know.

Carla   Do you?

Heather   Yes of course I do. I'm not a total innocent.

Carla   Alright.

Heather   I mean I know you remember me as a bit of a loser but I have lived a life since then. I've done stuff. I'm not squeaky clean.

Carla   I'll take your word for it. HEATHER: Gosh it still works doesn't it?

Carla   What does?

Heather   Your thing. That you do. I don't know. The face. The whole demeanor. It makes you seem so, I don't know, powerful.

Carla   If you like.

Heather   God it takes me back. I used to be terrified of you.

Carla   . . .

Heather   You used to have such a presence at school. It was pretty amazing because you weren't that big really. I mean I was definitely taller than you but I would never have tried to stand up to you. Never. The things you would say.

Carla   Look I don't even remember talking to you after year eight so whatever you think I did was probably someone else.

Heather   Probably. I mean, it's all in the past now anyway isn't it?

Carla   Yeh and I said I was sorry.

Heather   Yes you did.

Carla   So can we get on with this please?

Heather   Yes.

Carla   When do you want it done? I mean I reckon I could get everything ready in a couple of weeks.

Heather   Gosh. Two weeks!

Carla   I can't do it any sooner.

Heather   No of course. Two weeks is so imminent. I'd assume you'd have wanted to wait until . . . well . . . might I ask how you're going to manage doing all this with that?

Points to **Carla**'s *bump.*

Heather   Because I'd imagine it might get in the way. Or god forbid you knock it in some way. I don't want to be held responsible for the death of your unborn child.

Carla   Look don't worry. I can do this. Just leave that door open as if he's been outside for a fag and forgotten to lock up. I won't be climbing through windows or nothing.

Heather   But if he gets fighty.

Carla   He won't. I'll give him a good pounding on the head before he's even roused from his boozy sleep.

Heather   If all goes well.

Carla   It will.

Heather   I just think it's worth me pointing out at this juncture that I'm not going to be paying for any special needs schooling down the line. That's all I'm saying.

Carla   I hear you loud and clear.

Heather   And anyway I'm being practical and realistic.

This is a business transaction. I don't want it turned into anything else. And on that matter if you ever think up the bright idea of blackmailing me for more money once this is all done I will have no hesitation in taking you straight to the police station. If that means I'm imprisoned too then so be it. I won't go down without you.

Carla   Well done.

Heather   What?

Carla   Nice speech.

Heather   Oh fuck off.

Carla   I mean it. You've got the makings of a real hard nut.

Heather   And you've got the makings of a patronising bitch.

Carla   Looks like we're both a bit more like each other than we thought.

Pause in conversation. **Carla** *spots the insects on the wall.*

Carla   Whose are these? Yours or his?

Heather   His.

Carla   That is one nasty looking spider.

Heather   He didn't catch them himself. He bought all those off eBay. Framed in shit plastic frames and ready to hang.

Carla   Weird thing to have on your wall.

Heather   Yeh well that's Simon. Ever the enthusiast. Gets an interest in something, buys everything related to it, bores the back teeth off anyone who will listen then moves onto something else leaving massive indifference in his wake.

Carla   What's this one?

Heather   Which one?

Carla   This one.

Heather   Tarantula Hawk.

Carla   No this winged thing, like a wasp.

Heather   Yes it's a wasp called a Tarantula Hawk.

It's something he got a bit obsessed with after watching some documentary on TV.

Carla   Why 'tarantula'?

Heather   Because it preys on them.

Carla   Gutsy!

Heather   That was his favourite thing about them. It stings and paralyses them. Takes them to its lair. Plants an egg on it which burrows into it and grows feeding off its insides, but avoiding the major organs so it's still alive.

Carla   The tarantula?

Heather   Yeh. It needs it alive throughout its pupation.

And once it's fully grown it burrows out and the spider dies.

Carla   Dark.

Heather   Yep.

Carla   Bit like being pregnant.

Heather   What? Being eaten from the inside out?

Carla   May as well be. Wouldn't it be nice if once they're grown we mothers get to die and they have to head out and fend for themselves.

Heather   Is it really that bad?

Carla   I won't answer that. Nasty sting.

Heather   Yep. Simon revels in telling dinner guests what it feels like to be stung by one even though he's never even seen one alive.

Carla   What does it feel like?

Heather   Well according to Simon so therefore; according to Google, it is 'three minutes of intense pain whereby you can do absolutely nothing at all except scream'.

Carla   Intense.

Heather   But once the three minutes is up it's fine. Or at least better than before.

Carla   I kind of understand why Simon thinks they're cool.

Heather   I think they're vile. And Simon not only thinks they're cool but he also seems to believe that it means he is also cool by association. And he's about as far away from cool as he could be. He's like a fucking furnace of uncoolness. It's like he doesn't realise that being average at everything he fucking tries is absolutely nothing to fucking boast about. Just because he has a wide and varied field of interest doesn't make him a varied and interesting person. He does everything just enough to say that he's done it but he never fucking excels at anything. Of course he doesn't 'Oh I've done this' or 'I've been accepted as a member of such and such a club' but he's not the fucking president is he? He's not the fucking best in his field. No he's the one skulking in the corner, nursing his half pint of bitter and laughing his shitty high pitched laugh on the corner of conversations so that he can pretend he's part of them. Because he would never be in the middle of them because he has absolutely nothing of interest to say.

He's an average fucking pathetic fucking pointless little man. He's a complete and utter prick.

Carla   OK?

Heather   Sorry.

Carla   No, it's OK, you hate the bloke, you want him dead, I get it.

Heather   No you don't get it. This man is a serial adulterer.

He hoodwinks, lies and abuses. It's not just been one woman it's been several. I need you to know I've not taken this decision

lightly. It is for very good reason I want him dead. He's a
poisonous human being. He brings nothing but hurt to the world.

Carla   Sounds like as good a reason as any to kill a man.

No objections here.

Heather   This all feels very chummy doesn't it?

Carla   What?

Heather   Us. I sort of feel like we're getting on.

Carla   If you like.

Heather   It's funny I sort of didn't expect that we would.

We're so different.

Carla   Are we?

Heather   Yes we are.

Carla   Please yourself.

Heather   Do you know that I actually spent most of my teen
years quite severely depressed?

Carla   Didn't we all?

Heather   Well I suppose that it can be argued that all teenagers
are effectively depressed. Mentally imbalanced would be a fair
assessment. Yes. But I genuinely spent the majority of my days in
misery.

Carla   OK.

Heather   I just want you to know that.

Carla   You're saying it like it's my fault.

Heather   You don't think it's your fault?

Carla   No! Fuck no. We were all fucked up. It was school. I mean
come on. Everyone was horrible to everyone.

Heather   Not everyone.

Carla   Yes everyone. I dealt with shit too. That was part of it. We all had to go through it. You're nothing special Heather. It was fucked. Come on. I said I was sorry.

Heather   Two words twenty years after doesn't quite feel enough though does it?

Carla   Well I don't actually know what else I can do. You seem to think something specific happened that was me. I don't know what that was. So come on; what was it I did?

Heather   Really?

Carla   Yes. Other than the normal shit that everyone did.

You know the name calling. The, I don't know, the fucking teasing or a bit of a tussle. Other than that shit what did I do that has made you so fucking bitter?

Heather   Year seven residential. When we went to Wales. That's where it all began. Just after the pigeon. We left on the coach and we were friends and by the time we came home, three days later, we weren't. Do you remember why?

Carla   Fuck me, are you going to be able to tell me what I had for breakfast on that trip too?

Heather   You knew I liked Toby Mackenzie. I'd told you I liked Toby Mackenzie. So you went up to Toby in the field, just before we were due to play rounders, and you told Toby that I liked him and that you had seen me masturbating in the shower and that I'd told you I was thinking about him.

Carla   Jesus.

Heather   You told him this and then you turned around to me and you looked me in the eye and said 'You're disgusting and I don't want to share a room with you no more'.

Carla   It was year seven! You do shit things like that in year seven!

Heather   I spent the rest of my school years being known as 'Dirty Heather'. That became 'Leather Heather' when people worked out what S&M stood for and decided that I would probably be into that. Everyone thought I was some kind of sex addict which could have been kind of cool if it wasn't for the fact that everyone thought I was physically revolting. It would have worked out fine if I'd been good looking. Wouldn't it? But it didn't. I spent every lunch time in the art room with Ms Beacher and every break making sure I avoided you and your gang. But I didn't always manage to did I?

Carla   I didn't come here to be fucking lectured right? If you don't shut the fuck up I'm leaving and your plan to kill your husband yeh? Your plan will be round town as fast as you can say 'Dirty fucking Heather' so you shut your mouth.

Heather   You wouldn't do that because you need the money.

Carla   Not this much. I don't. Fuck you and your stupid trip down memory lane. I ain't doing this no more.

Heather   Yes you fucking are because you owe it to me and you know it.

Carla   I owe you nothing.

Heather   Do you really believe that? Is that what you think?

This isn't about Toby. Don't you remember what came after?

Carla *goes up very close to* **Heather**'s *face.*

Carla   I know what it is you're getting at. Don't worry sweetheart. And I can tell you now; that was one of the most satisfying moments of my life.

Heather *is trying to hold her nerve.*

Carla   You thought you were so much better than me. You had your mum and dad at your beck and call. Anything you wanted. School work was easy. Teacher pleaser. Neat fucking uniform. Goody fucking two shoes. And I'd been waiting to wipe that smile off your face for years. You didn't know. You didn't fucking know what my life had been like and you judged me every day. The day I killed the pigeon you want to know what had happened that

morning? I'll tell you what had happened. I had watched my dad
smack my mum round the face so hard her eye popped out. Clean
out of its socket. I watched her put it back in while I called an
ambulance. That's just the kind of thing he did. Most days. And
pretty soon it wasn't just mum it was me as well. So when I used to
go round yours and see what life you had at first it was like a
fucking refuge for me. They were nice and stuff. I liked being
there. It was all so calm. But then I started to realise that actually
the longer I spend with you and your perfect sunshine family the
more my family looks like a black hole of shit. And then your face
when I killed the pigeon. The shock. You knew fuck all. You were
still a child and even though we were the same age I was an adult
already. I couldn't be your friend. You pissed me off. You didn't
know anything. You didn't understand why I'd done it. And even if
I'd explained to you then and there; you still wouldn't have
understood. Would you?

Heather   No.

Carla   So there you go. Can I go now? I feel like this has reached
a natural fucking end.

Heather   I knew about your dad. I'd seen your bruises. I knew
also cos my mum wouldn't let me go and stay at yours and I had
wanted to know why. I didn't have anything I could say to make
that better. But I thought that if I was your friend. And we could do
nice things together. And my family became a place you could
come to. Then that's what I could do.

Carla   You knew about my dad? Your mum knew?

Heather   Yes.

Carla   And she did nothing?

Heather   God I don't know do I? Maybe she did? Maybe she
called social services or I don't know, spoke to your mum. I was
too young.

Carla   I was too young.

Heather   Yeh well. So was I.

Beat.

Carla   You must have known it was coming.

Heather   Of course I did. I'd spent the weeks up to it in complete terror.

Carla   Well that's school for you.

Heather   . . .

Carla   Training ground for life.

Heather   I was so confused about it all. Do you remember me trying to talk to you about it? Every time I tried to get you on your own so we could speak as friends, like we had been, every time you would blank me. We'd been friends, Carla.

Pause.

Heather   I'd never even been slapped let alone punched before that day. I couldn't see out of my left eye for two weeks it was so swollen. It was such a shock. Came out of the sky almost. One minute I'm walking, next I'm on the floor. But for all the pain I was in it was the idea that you did it. We'd been friends. I didn't name you when they asked. I knew that you could have been expelled.

Carla   Am I supposed to say thank you?

They stare at each other. **Carla** *sways slightly.* **Heather** *notices and checks her watch.*

Carla   Are we going to finish talking about the plan or can I leave?

Heather   Let's finish.

They collect themselves.

Carla   Right. So. You get him pissed. Call me. Leave the back door open. I come round. I bosh him. Take some stuff and leave. Sound about right?

Heather   I guess.

Carla   No 'I guess', I want certainty. This has to go perfectly.

Heather   Of course.

Carla   And when do we do the rest of the money?

Heather   When it's done.

Carla   I want half up front now.

Heather   Not possible.

Carla   Make it possible.

Heather   It's ten thousand pounds. My bank won't release that in cash just like that. Anyway you've already had ten grand. That should be enough to keep you going.

Carla   It's not about that you idiot. You should be taking it out in smaller amounts gradually. So they can't track it.

Heather   Really?

Carla   Yes really. Fucksake. Right look. After this we'll go to the cashpoint and you take out the most you can and give it to me today. Do the same tomorrow. Then leave it a few days and do the same. By the time it's all done I'll have had a fair chunk and then you can give me the rest in two installments. How does that sound?

Heather   Sounds very organised.

Carla   One other thing.

Heather   What?

Carla   I don't know what the fucker looks like. You don't seem to keep photos around the place of each other do you? Just dead wasps and shit pain'tings. What's he look like?

Heather *pauses and just regards* **Carla** *for a moment. She checks her watch again.* **Carla** *sways again.*

Carla   Heather? Photo?

Heather *takes in a deep breath and lets it out calmly.*

Heather   I made you a little pack of photos and information.

Carla   Organised!

Heather   It's in the desk over there. Under my laptop.

You grab it and I'll tidy up. He'll be home soon. I don't want him to know I've had a guest.

Carla *turns away from* **Heather** *to go to the desk. As soon as she does* **Heather** *calmly and efficiently pulls surgical gloves from her pocket and puts them on. She removes from her other pocket a small vial of liquid and a handkerchief that she dispenses the liquid onto. CARLA meanwhile has found the file and is looking at the photos. She has gone very quiet. She stands staring at the photos in her hand. Back still to* **Heather**. **Heather** *is ready now and is simply standing, watching* **Carla** *and waiting. Eventually . . .*

Carla   This is . . . I mean . . . this . . .

Carla *still stands with her back to* **Heather**. **Carla** *sways again.*

Heather   The man in the photo you are looking at is . . .

Carla   It's James.

Carla *is slurring a bit when she speaks.*

Heather   No. His name is Simon. James is a pseudonym. You must know that most men who visit prostitutes don't want to use their real name. Identification aside I suppose it's also a means of separating their deed from their real life. That is Simon and he is my husband. As you know he's been visiting you for a couple of years now and crucially he was visiting you quite heavily around seven months ago, wouldn't you agree?

Carla   Yes.

Heather   I'm not sure your tea has completely taken effect.

Carla   What?

Heather   Apologies for what I'm about to do.

Carla   What are you about to do?

In one step **Heather** *very quickly grabs* **Carla** *who is still looking at the photos and processing what's going on, places the handkerchief over her mouth and holds it there as* **Carla** *struggles.*

Blackout.

Act Three

Heather's *living room as before.* **Carla** *is sitting on a chair, hands and feet bound to the chair with plastic ties. She is gagged.* **Heather** *is watching her, checks the time then produces some kind of smelling salt and waves it under* **Carla**'s *nose. This rouses* **Carla** *though not instantly. As she comes to* **Heather** *settles down with the paper on her lap and pours herself a cup of tea from a set on the table. There is a sense that* **Heather** *is staging this action for effect. She reacts aggressively when she realises what is happening but is too restrained to have an effect.*

Heather   Don't knock yourself backwards love, you'll smack your head.

Carla *looks at* **Heather** *with wide angry eyes.*

Heather   You've had a proper snooze, do you feel a bit better now? It's been lovely for me. I've had a bit of a tidy up and a potter around. I like to imagine this would be what it's like with a young baby. Them taking their naps while I get on with the housework. Is that how it is? Happy scenes of domesticity? Or is it fraught mayhem as you try and keep on top of everything including your sanity? I mean I have kept up with your Facebook updates on such things and it does seem that on a day-to-day basis things do change quite often. One day you may be blissfully in love with your 'babies' and thanking god for this precious gift and the next you're wishing you'd never had any fucking kids and that someone would come and take them the fuck away. It must be so trying. I can only imagine. I mean before the internet how did mothers vent? I suppose to their girlfriends, but what about the 2 a.m. posts during a sleepless night? Would mothers have simply cursed at the walls?

Would they have nudged their partners awake to give them a pithy couple of sentences that humourously gave insight into their exhausted exasperation? And what about single mothers? Who would they have spoken to? It must have been so hard. I mean it must still be so hard. But it also must be worth it. This creature. This thing. Loving you. Needing you.

She drinks some tea and sits thinking. **Carla** *seems frozen, unsure what to do.*

Heather   I got to a point where I thought there was something wrong with my body. We'd had ourselves checked of course and nothing was showing up but I knew for absolute certain that there was something going on. Like a switch hadn't been flicked. And I remember my mother saying to me that getting pregnant involved a whole lot of alchemy. That my body was in charge and actually I couldn't force it or will it on. My body would decide when the right time was. And this was the single most horrendous thing for me to deal with because I felt like I had no control over it. It was a problem I couldn't solve. But looking back on it all now I know exactly why it wasn't working. Do you remember the year nine disco?

Carla *just stares at her.*

Heather   I wasn't going to go but by then I'd made friends with Ruth and that lot and they encouraged me I guess.

I wasn't going to go. I mean it was less than a year since you smashed my face in the school corridor and I was still suffering from panic attacks so my parents didn't want me to but I really, really wanted to be normal. I really, really wanted to be a normal teenager. You know? Going out. Doing the odd naughty thing. Staying with friends. So actually the plan was I would go for a couple of hours and then I would call mum and let her know if I either wanted picking up straight away or if I was happy I would stay longer. And the first couple of hours were fine weren't they? Because you weren't there. So I said to Mum, don't worry, pick me up at ten. And went back to dancing with my friends. But then you turned up. With the others. And I immediately wished I was no longer there. My friends were good but ineffective. They were as scared of you as I was. I was a pretty good shield for them. And the teachers were hopeless as they probably all wanted to go home and were busy doing the bare minimum they could.

She pauses for a moment. Recalling. **Carla** *is still.*

Heather   Those toilets. Black. Why no lights? All of us in there. The four of you, then the other three, can't remember them but along for the ride, then me. Crammed in but I don't think I've ever felt so alone. She said . . . who was that? . . . Was it Beth? Was it Beth?

Looks to **Carla**. **Carla** *doesn't move.*

Heather   Whoever. She said. 'Strip'. You see last time, in the corridor, it was just ambush. It was just violence. I say 'just' but. It was just trying to hurt my body. So this time. I don't know man, what was it? You were wanting to hurt me but it was different. She said 'strip'. And I did. 'Open your legs, stand wide'. And I did. I think there were three girls behind me not doing anything, just watching. Not sure how they felt about it all but they wouldn't have rocked the boat. You and Beth and Joanne and Kerry were steering. I closed my eyes. It went very quiet. Then something went up and in. I mean not smoothly. Not just like that. You had to really feel around and get it in there. Shove it in. What was it? I don't even know, to this day, what it was you put in. What was it?

She looks at **Carla**.

Heather   I'll remove the gag shortly. I will give you a chance to answer. I just want some space for my words first. Up and in. And then you all just stood there looking at me.

In the strange half light of the toilets. The skylight letting in some of the moon. Shadows making your faces seem more. I don't know. Strange. Laughing. And then it sort of petered out. And that's when you walked over to me, pulled out the object and whispered in my ear. Do you remember what you said?

She looks at **Carla**.

Heather   'Good girl'. And then you were gone. It was as if I had performed well. As if I had done exactly as I was supposed to. And I felt. I felt.

She wobbles. Then regains.

Heather   I put my clothes back on. I left. I waited on the road until ten o'clock and my mum picked me up. I didn't tell her. I didn't tell anyone. I acted as if nothing had happened. And for some reason that worked. You didn't do anything to me again. It was as if you'd got what you wanted. What had you got? It was weird. It was fucking weird. But you seemed happy. I can't believe you didn't think that what you'd done to me at school was bad. Had you forgotten? How could you have forgotten?

She pauses.

Heather   OK. So I was talking about trying for a baby.

And it got onto that. So. OK. What I meant was that even though there was nothing wrong with my body. I should technically be able to do it. Even though that was the case. I knew that I wouldn't because of that night. I could feel what I would describe as a blockage. Do you get that? I feel blocked up. Or maybe like a splinter that is in the perfect position to block something's way. A dam. A shut door. A log in the road. And actually whatever it was had some kind of fucking life to it. Like I feel life inside me. I mean this is fucked up but inside me I feel like there's this growth. It's growing. Not unlike, I assume, a baby. Or a tumour. Or a parasite. And I've had the scans. There's nothing there. But for me there is. A phantom growth if you like. It's really, really there. And recently I've been trying to work out a way to release it.

She stares hard at **Carla**. *She breathes. Then stands up.*

Heather (*brisk*)   So what I'm going to do now is remove the gag around your mouth. This is your opportunity to speak. If you try to scream or shout the gag will be replaced and you will not get the opportunity again. Do you understand? Nod if you do.

Carla *doesn't move.*

Heather   I said do you understand? I want to see a nod.

Carla *doesn't move.*

Heather   SHOW ME A FUCKING NOD OR I WILL KILL YOU RIGHT NOW.

Carla *nods.*

Heather (*calm again*)   Good. Removing it now.

She takes the gag off. **Carla** *looks like she's going to explode but* **Heather** *gives her a look and she says nothing.*

Heather   Do you have anything to say?

A long pause as **Carla** *collects herself and tries to think.*

Carla   Are you going to kill me?

Heather   Next question.

Carla   Are you going to kill me?

Heather   Next question.

Carla   It won't help you. With whatever fucked up mental problem you have you fucking insane ass psycho. It won't help you. All it will do is get you into prison and then you'll have more fucking problems than you do already. So take it from me yeh don't fucking kill me yeh? Don't kill me.

Heather   Thanks for the advice. Anything else?

Carla   I just want to say yeh that, listen right . . .

Heather   I'm listening.

Carla (*starting to get worked up*)   Because actually this is all just too fucking much yeh? Cos like I said sorry and I was like really sorry but I was fucked up myself and I ain't excusing it yeh cos I know what I did was shit but I mean I wish I could go back and like not do it or something but the thing is yeh that I had stuff going on like I said before and I didn't know what I was doing and I didn't know right from wrong and I'm sorry I am I'm really really sorry and I just don't know what else to say but please don't hurt me or my baby yeh? Please.

Heather   Gosh.

Carla   Please.

Carla *is weeping a bit now.*

Heather   Well that was a bit unexpected.

Carla   Don't hurt me.

Heather   I can't believe I've actually made Carla Jackson cry.

Carla   Please.

Heather   I almost want to do a Facebook update.

Carla   Look you've got what you wanted. You got me to cry and say sorry. I get it. I was a bitch. You had a hard time. I want to go now please.

Heather   Ah now, no that won't be possible.

Carla   Why?

Heather   Because I'm not done.

Carla   Oh god you're going to kill me aren't you? Oh god.

Heather   Actually you almost derailed all of this when we first met. When you offered me your child.

Carla   You want my child?

Heather   Perhaps.

Carla   You can have it. You can. I'll take the money and as soon as it's born it's yours.

Heather   . . .

Carla   Don't kill me.

Heather   You'd give away your child for your life.

Carla   You think I'm stupid? You've done the sums. I know you know. Is he in on it too? Is he listening somewhere?

Heather   Who?

Carla   Simon. He sent you to do his dirty work? You can't have kids together so you get some slag pregnant and steal it?

Heather   . . .

Carla   It's his kid Heather. You know it and I know it. So if you want the fucking thing then it's yours.

Pause.

Heather   How can you be sure?

Carla   I'm sure.

Heather   Are you? I mean, how can you be? You're forgetting I've been watching you. Simon wasn't your only client.

Carla   He was the only one who paid for no rubber.

Heather   . . .

Carla   It's his.

Heather   And not your husband's?

Carla   We ain't had sex in years. He only thinks it's his because I told him we'd done it when he was drunk.

Heather   Oh sweetheart! Whatever he's promised you he would never have intended on giving. I did tell you what a massive prick he was. He can't be the first one to make big promises to you.

Carla   He isn't.

Heather   So really you should perhaps get better at not taking them seriously.

Carla   Yeh.

Heather   So look this has all got a bit, I don't know, chummy again. The fact is that the plan was to ask you for your child but the plan was also to get an apology out of you.

Both of these things seem to have been resolved so really I should let you go and we can organise the practicalities around adopting the baby.

Carla   Yes.

Heather   Not really as simple as that actually.

Carla   Why?

Heather   Because I can still feel it. Inside me. And I've been waiting for it do something, to hatch, to escape, to burst from me, to dissipate, whatever it is. I've been waiting so long. And nothing I've done has worked. None of this has worked. It's why I'm thinking I should be doing something more drastic.

Carla   Look. When we first met up you were on about violence. This isn't you Heather. This isn't your world. Why are you doing this?

Heather   Isn't this sad?

Carla   What?

Heather   I used to really really like you. I really thought we were best friends. God I wish I could find some empathy somewhere. I know that's what I'm supposed to do. I know I should be looking at your background and excusing your behaviour as a symptom. I was just caught in the crossfire wasn't I? And yet I can't let go of this need to hurt you. I get it. I'm a hypocrite. I kind of feel like I'm OK with that though. So here's the thing. What if I told you that Simon was dead already?

Carla   What?

Heather   That I'd hacked him to death in a bit of a jealous rage and he is currently in the freezer until I work out what to do with him.

Carla   . . .

Heather *produces a knife.*

Heather   And what if I also told you that I was planning on using this knife to extract the baby from your stomach whilst you were still alive so you could watch me take it out of you and cradle it in front of you before you bled to death?

Carla   . . .

Heather   Because I find that sometimes it creates greater impact and anticipation if you pre-bill your intentions. So. What do you think? How do you feel about all that?

Carla   I think you're fucking insane.

Heather   Potentially.

Carla   You can't cut the baby out. You don't know what you're doing. You might hurt it. It's not ready to come out. What if it doesn't survive?

Heather   You said yourself you don't want the child.

What's the problem?

Carla   The problem? You're going to kill me! It's going to fucking hurt! I don't want to die! What's wrong with you? Oh god what is going on? What the hell is all this? I wish I'd never fucking met up with you. I should have left when I could have. This is a nightmare. You're a nightmare.

What the fuck is going on?

Heather   It's all very weird isn't it?

Carla   I don't understand why you're doing this.

Heather   You see? There is an impact to everything a person does. Even the simplest moment. Even a single word can have an effect. It could be that this has only a very miniscule effect or it could be bigger. I just kind of wish we could all be nicer to each other.

Carla   You call this being nice? This is nice? You're insane! Let me go! LET ME GO! SOMEONE HELP ME! HELP ME!

Heather *quickly gags* **Carla** *again.* **Carla** *struggles. We see liquid spreading through her trousers from her crotch. She's pissed herself.*

Heather *sees it and doesn't say anything.* **Carla** *looks down at the floor.* **Heather** *walks over to the coffee table where her phone is. She checks a text message she's received. She pauses, thinking. She makes a decision.*

Heather (*softly*)   I've always found the idea of revenge repulsive. I find the threat of violence worse. I feel it is a sign of weakness in

a person. Like an adult who hits a child. I don't view it as a valid
form of discipline. It is a failing on the part of the adult. They
should find ways to decipher why the child is acting up and to
tackle that with words. With encouragement. With love. I am of
course saying this from the point of view of a woman who has
never had children of her own. I understand how this disqualifies
me from being allowed an opinion on such things. I'm sure you
disagree with me. I'm sure you'll say that sometimes you need to
give a child a short sharp smack in order to get their attention.
Perhaps they're in danger. Perhaps they have done something
dangerous to someone else. Whatever it is I'm sure you could
justify it. But in my eyes violence is violence is violence. And I'm
really very worried about the world that this child is about to be
introduced into. There seems to be no solution to violence other
than more violence. And it is for this that I am to do what I am
going to do. I really want you to understand that I don't hate you
for what you did. In fact I completely and unreservedly accept your
apology. I was being dramatic before, I do have some empathy for
your situation even if I don't think it excuses your behaviour. But
I'm afraid that I don't think you have yet been able to understand
just how much of an impact you had on me. I have thought many
times about how to resolve this problem. This, whatever it is inside
me. I really wanted it to be solved with something beautiful. So
much of me wanted to be able to get pregnant so that I could pour
all my remaining love into a child and it would in some way create
a new start. I could try to ensure it had a better beginning than me.
So much of me wanted to find a love with a man that would render
all my past experiences with human beings forgettable. Someone
who could make everything better. A human plaster. But none of
these things happened and in fact when I found out what Simon
had been doing and looked further into it and realised it was you I
just think that something really simple happened. My body
emptied of any kind of joy. Any kind of hope. And I found out
what it was to hate. And now I know why so many people do the
things that they do. I hope you'll understand. There are choices we
must all make based on instinct, experience and knowledge. Of
course we can't always make the right ones, we're only human
after all, but for the most part one hopes that the majority of people

will be motivated by a sense of kindness towards other human beings. You'd hope. I think the problem is that actually we're taught that this isn't the way to get what we want. Kindness and care is a pathetic way of going about things. Want to get what you want? Kick the fucking door in. And we're taught this by people who learnt the hard way. They learnt what it feels like to be defeated and it's made them want to defeat. I know not everyone is like this but too many are. Too many with true power are. And so now we're fucked. Because the cycle just creates more and more people who think like this. I mean hell, even I have started thinking like this. I'd really like to stop this cycle. I really would. But there's something inside me saying that kindness won't work. Not with you. Unless I've got it wrong. Have I got it wrong? Have I got you wrong?

She puts the knife down on the floor and takes the gag off **Carla**'s *mouth.*

Heather   I'm going to undo the hand and foot ties.

I'm trusting you not to run. I'm hoping you'll understand that what I'm doing is for us all.

Carla *says nothing as* **Heather** *takes scissors and cuts the plastic ties.* **Heather** *steps away. The knife is between* **Carla** *and* **Heather** *on the floor.* **Heather** *sees* **Carla** *look at it.* **Carla** *stands. They are equal distance from it.*

Heather   I'm sorry your dad did what he did to you and your mum.

Carla   Thank you.

Heather   I'm sorry you had such a shitty upbringing.

Carla   Thank you.

Heather   I'm sorry you've since had a bit of a crappy life.

Carla   It's not been as bad as you think.

Heather   I really wish things had been different.

Carla   You killed Simon?

Heather   . . .

Carla   I don't understand. You don't like violence but you do it. You think that it's wrong but you do it. I don't get what it is I'm supposed to be learning. You hate revenge but you're doing it. Why am I here? Do you feel better now? Are you going to kill me and then feel better? Are you going to rip my baby from me and then feel better?

I may have been violent in the past but I've never been this premeditated. Even when I was at my worst at school I never thought about it this much. I don't know why I would do it. I mean we're animals right? My instincts kick in.

Carla *is slowly, inch by inch, getting closer to the knife.*

Carla   I'm not sure that your version, all reasoned out, all justified in your head is better than mine. I'm acting on impulse. You've planned it. You've been talking about this thing inside you growing. I know what it is. Everyone has it. It's fucking disappointment. It's a massive fucking sense that actually everything life was supposed to be is never going to happen and in fact it's going to be worse than you ever imagined. I got it much younger than you. And it's still there. You're no different to me. You're no different to anyone.

Heather   Not everyone feels like that.

Carla   Yeh everyone does.

Heather   No they don't. And they only feel like that when something happens to them. Something horrible. And even then most people are able to outweigh that with good things. Great things that happen.

Carla   Then they're living a fantasy. That's not life.

Heather   It's self-perpetuating. You hurt so you must hurt.

You don't get to be happy so no one else must. It's horrible.

Carla   You're doing it too.

Heather   Am I?

Carla   You don't think that what you're doing is the same?

Heather   No.

Carla   Then you're more insane than I thought you were.

Carla *is very close to the knife now.*

Heather   I want you to think really carefully about what your instincts are telling you right now. I want you to think about your baby. I want you to think about your other children.

I want you to make a decision based on everything that has happened. Right back to when we were kids. Right up to now. I have threatened you with death. I have told you I want to take your child from you. I have told you I have killed the man you thought was going to help you get away from your life. I have not done anything violent towards you yet but I have suggested to you that I will. I want you to listen to everything that is happening in your head and your heart right now. Is it to be kindness or violence?

Carla   I don't understand!

Heather   By freeing you I have given you two opportunities. Kindness or violence? Which one are you going to choose?

Carla   What are you about to do?

Heather   What are you going to choose?

Carla   What have you got in your hands?

Heather   Make your choice.

Carla   Show me your hands. SHOW ME YOUR HANDS.

Heather *shows* **Carla** *she is holding the scissors.* **Carla** *takes a beat to decide then grabs the knife and plunges it into* **Heather***'s chest. They stand connected to each other via the blade breathing.* **Heather***'s breath is faltering with pain. They look at each other.* **Heather** *smiles.*

Carla   Why are you smiling?

Offstage we hear the sound of a key in the lock of **Heather**'s *front door.*

Carla   Who's that?

The door opens and shuts and we hear someone taking their coat off.

Carla   Who's that?

Simon (*offstage*)   Heather?

Carla *looks at* **Heather**.

Carla   You said he was dead.

Simon (*offstage*)   You home?

Carla   What the fuck is going on?

Heather *smiles at her.*

Carla   What have you done? They'll think it was all me.

Heather what have you done?

Heather (*whispers*)   Good girl.

Carla   What did you say?

Heather (*louder*)   Good girl.

Heather *collapses onto her. Just as the living room door starts to get pushed open the lights snap to black.*

Mum

Morgan Lloyd Malcolm

Mum was originally co-produced by Francesca Moody Productions, Soho Theatre, Theatre Royal Plymouth, and Popcorn Group. It was first performed on 30 September 2021 at Theatre Royal Plymouth with the following cast and creative team:

Nina	Sophie Melville
Jackie	Cat Simmons
Pearl	Denise Black

Creative Team

Writer: Morgan Lloyd Malcolm
Director: Abigail Graham
Set and Costume Designer: Sarah Beaton
Lighting Designer: Sally Ferguson
Sound Designer: Anna Clock
Movement Director: Annie-Lunnette Deakin-Foster
Associate Director: T.D. Moyo
Artists Wellbeing Practitioner: Lou Platt
Associate Producer: Kater Gordon
Company Stage Manager: Caoimhe Regan

For all our mums

Nina *stands on the shore. Looking out to sea. She is pregnant. She is wrapped in a towel. She has just been for a swim. She is happy. The sound of the waves is overwhelming and womblike.*

Nina *suddenly changes. A violent and scary shift.*

Nina's *house. A sitting room.* **Nina** *stands in the middle of the room, no longer pregnant, arms outstretched to the door. She has just given something away that she may never get back. Suddenly* **Pearl** *bursts in the room. It makes* **Nina** *jump and drop her arms.*

Pearl   Sorry darlin', I checked the bag and realised I think I left the new pack of dummies you gave me in the kitchen, I won't be a mo.

She exits in a different direction. **Nina** *watches her go. After a moment* **Pearl** *returns with dummies.*

Pearl   I'd forget my head if it weren't screwed on. You OK, love?

Nina *doesn't answer.*

Pearl   Oh look, he'll be fine. David's getting him in the car seat right now and he's as happy as Larry. And like I said, if at any point we think he needs to see his mum we'll bring him straight back. But he won't. I want you to try and rest tonight, OK? This is for you. You're exhausted and this is a well earned break. Will Jackie be here soon?

Nina   Eight.

Pearl   Well, why don't you run a bath. Bit of me-time, eh? And don't you fret, I'll be right there to help David. He has back up! It'll be lovely for everyone. And we'll get him back to you in the morning not too early. You've been doing so well, Nina. We're all so proud of you.

She gives **Nina** *a big hug.* **Nina** *sinks into it.*

Pearl   Your mum would be too. Rest up darlin'. You're too hard on yourself. He'll be back in your arms in no time.

Pearl *leaves.* **Nina** *stands arms outstretched from the hug towards the door.*

She has been holding her breath and suddenly realises and exhales then sobs with a sharp intake of breath but stops herself.

A ringing in all our ears.

Nina   Oh!

A knocking that seems distant at first then becomes louder and more insistent as if creeping into **Nina***'s consciousness.*

Jackie *enters.*

Jackie   I'm looking for my friend Nina, does she live here anymore?

Nina   What time is it?

Jackie   The neighbours were saying they kept seeing a little pale face at the window mouthing 'Help me! What have I done?' I thought I should investigate.

Nina   Sorry, he's only just gone. I haven't had a chance to clean up. Did you bring wine?

Jackie   Of course I brought wine. I'm not a fucking savage. Glasses?

Nina   Like you don't know where they are.

Jackie   Feisty. Alright! We'll order food. You OK?

Nina   Yes, of course I am! I'm free! Fucking hell, mate. I mean fucking hell.

Jackie   That bad?

Nina   No. Yes. No. It's the most intense thing I think I've ever experienced. You must hear this all the time but oh my god, what is going on? I didn't know I could both love and hate something so fully, with my whole body. Not hate him, no, not hate him. Hate the, I guess, hate the experience you know? But also LOVE him so much. Love it all. It's everything they, you, said it would be but more. And you can't comprehend that until you're in the middle of it, can you? I couldn't prepare myself for any of this. Who could?

Jackie   You can't.

Nina   I promise I won't talk about him all night.

Jackie   I can't believe I haven't met him yet.

Nina   Me neither.

Jackie   I should have come earlier but my shift ran over.

Nina   Am I being selfish? I'm being selfish.

Jackie   What?

Nina   I should be prioritising him, shouldn't I? Why have I let David take him?

Jackie   Drink.

Nina *downs the whole glass in one.*

Jackie   Oh hi there.

Nina   More.

Jackie   Shall we order that pizza?

Nina   Yes.

Jackie   I'll do it.

Jackie *fiddles with her phone doing the food order during the following.*

Nina   Most mothers don't do this. They just muddle through. They don't get breaks. Is this a cop out?

Jackie   No.

Nina   I should have just had David sleep with him in the spare room while I put some ear plugs in. Why did he have to take him to his mum's? I should call him back.

Jackie   No you fucking shouldn't. I've been looking forward to this night for ages. Pepperoni meat feast or four cheeses?

Nina   Both.

Jackie   And you need this. You need this so much. Take it. Honestly, the amount of mums who would kill for this.

Nina   Yeh.

Jackie   This is a good thing. He's not bringing him back too early tomorrow, is he?

Nina   No.

Jackie   Good. Sleep in. Lie in bed. Kick back tonight then rest. Seriously.

Nina   OK.

Jackie   And garlic bread. Done. So. Shall I tell you a secret?

Nina   Yes.

Jackie   Everyone feels like you do.

Nina   No they don't.

Jackie   They do.

Nina   They don't. I've met other mums with same age babies. They have their shit together. They've come out to rhyme time with spare clothes for the massive poonami during Wind The Bobbin Up. They've got a Bugaboo that's easy to push and they didn't think they could save some cash on some piece of crap buggy on ebay with no raincover. They don't turn up at coffee mornings with a baby who has no socks on because they forgot. In fact, they can stay at coffee mornings because their babies let them. Because they sleep. In their prams. Even if the pram isn't moving. I mean, what the fuck?! How is that even possible? And they have routines and shit. I can't even remember when I'm supposed to brush my teeth anymore. They don't Google shit. I Google everything. He cries, I Google 'why is he crying' and oh my god the amount of reasons it could be so what's the point? I'm shit at this. Aren't I supposed to be the one person who knows what to do for him? Isn't that, like, number one on the job description list? Know your baby's needs? He cries, I feed him, I change him, I cuddle him, he still cries. I mean. What? What the fuck, baby?

What do you want from me? What is it you actually need? And I didn't realise how tired it was possible to be without dying. Like, how am I not dead yet? How is no one in this house dead? I get it actually. I get the shaking thing. I had to put him down in the middle of the bed and walk away the other day. I get why people shake their babies. Because nothing makes any fucking sense about them and it's just so hard to know what else to do!

Jackie   Mate, it's OK.

Nina   I don't shake him so don't worry.

Jackie   I'm not worried.

Nina   I really don't.

Jackie   I know.

Nina   I've come close. I'll tell you that.

Jackie   You're only three months in. This is normal.

Nina   I'd never hurt him. I love him. Of course I do. I love him so much. It's unbearable sometimes. And I hold him. And I swaddle him. And I change him. And I feed him. And I do everything. Because of course I love him. I know I do. But also this love is just. It's just overwhelming. It's too much. And he won't sleep. I always thought people with babies who didn't sleep were just doing a shit job of not understanding what they were supposed to be doing and that if they were a good parent they would know. I thought I would know. Why won't he sleep?

Jackie   Babies don't sleep.

Nina   I know babies who sleep.

Jackie   Well, they're not normal and their mums are probably lying.

Nina   When you visit your mums after birth are they as bad as me?

Jackie   Most people are shattered shadows of their former selves.

Nina   Why don't people tell you this?

Jackie   I did.

Nina   I know but not really. Not this. You said it would be hard but you didn't say it would be like this. Like this. This is so hard I don't think I can actually do it. It's not even like I've hit a wall because I've hit so many walls since he arrived that I must be in a death maze of walls. In the last three months I've had two nights where I've slept longer than a three hour stretch and mostly I've been woken two hourly. How is that good? How is that a good idea?

Jackie   It isn't.

Nina   So what the fuck do I do?

Jackie   Is this your first evening to yourself?

Nina   This is the first time I've managed to feel OK with him going away with a bottle. I'm not actually OK with it but David said that he wanted to do it.

Jackie   You're going to be OK. This bit isn't forever.

Nina   But. It's twenty-four hours a day. Twenty-four hours. It's seven days a week. Even now, with him away with David, I'm on call. Because if anything happens he'll need me. With any other job you can work long hours and say to yourself 'Just get through this week and you can sleep on the weekend'. There is no weekend with kids. There is no weekend.

Jackie   How was the birth? Do you want to talk about that?

Nina   Not really. I didn't get you over here to counsel me. Fuck! I'm so sorry. I said I wouldn't talk about him and I've just vomited words at you. I'm sorry, Jacks. I want to have fun. So let's have fun. Come on! Like before. Let's get pissed and dance around. Let's talk about cock and what you're getting. What are you getting? Who's your current one?

Jackie   Still Kenny.

Nina   How many months has that been then?

Jackie   A year.

Nina   Oh my god, I've been so fucking up my own uterus I've not even noticed. This is good news though, right? You like him?

Jackie   Yeh.

Nina   So, is this *the* guy then?

Jackie   I hope so.

Nina   I want to meet him!

Jackie   You will. In fact – he's started swimming with me, maybe you could come with us.

Nina   Oh god.

Jackie   You miss it?

Nina   I do.

Jackie   Then come.

Nina   How? I barely have time to dress myself.

Jackie   Bring Ben with you and I'll hang out with him while you swim.

Nina   It's the logistics.

Jackie   It doesn't need to be hard.

Nina   I don't know why but it feels it.

Jackie   You'd got yourself to a really good place before, hadn't you?

Nina   Yes.

Jackie   The swims were helping.

Nina   Yes.

Jackie   Let's make it happen.

Nina   Do you remember when I was a laugh?

Jackie   This is all temporary.

Nina   It feels interminable.

Jackie   You spoken to anyone about it?

Nina   No. Because. Well, the thing is that when they come to check on you they are looking for whether you're coping or not. And if you're not then what happens then?

Jackie   They get you some help.

Nina   No, they take your baby away.

Jackie   They don't.

Nina   They could. Like if I say – yeh, I love him but he won't let me sleep and all I can think about is the many different horrible violent things that could happen to him on a loop. Or that I have to try really hard to stop myself from imagining the worst possible thing just as I go to sleep. Or that the acknowledgement that I am now in charge of his safety forever and ever is just simply too much. It's too much. Or if I tell them that I'm, that my, that everything I did before, all the work I put in before, it's all unravelling. If I tell them that then they will be worried and I don't want to worry them. So I pretend I'm fine.

Jackie   If you're not OK then you need to say.

Nina   I am though. I'm fine.

Jackie   Really?

Nina   Yes. Of course I am.

Jackie   All those things you just said . . .

Nina   That's just me though, isn't it? That's what I do? I'm fine. It's just hard. It's really hard.

Jackie   I'm glad we're doing this.

Nina *laughs at her.*

Jackie   I am!

Nina   How are you not running out the fucking door?

Jackie   You forget I've seen you in worse states than this.

Nina I don't think you have.

Jackie Many, many times. Holding your hair back. Hosing you down. Fuck head.

Nina Receipts!

Jackie I have so many. This is normal.

Nina At least that was self inflicted.

Jackie You chose to have a baby!

Nina I was misled! I would never have signed up to this.

Jackie Yeh, you would. Ben's so worth it.

Nina *doesn't answer.*

Nina Is he nice though? Your guy? Tell me he's nice.

Jackie He's nice.

Nina Swim or not, I want to meet him.

Jackie You will.

She suddenly seems to phase out and stare at nothing. **Jackie** *waits a moment expecting her to say something.*

Jackie Nina?

Nina *doesn't respond. She is staring. Eventually she mutters something under her breath.*

Nina Forget my head.

Jackie Nina, are you OK, love?

Nina *seems to snap out of it.*

Nina Yes. Sorry.

Jackie You're beginning to worry me, Ni.

Nina I'm fine. More booze? Where's that pizza?

Jackie Do you do that a lot?

Nina   Honestly I'm fine. He's not even messaged to say that things are OK. I mean that would be the kind thing to do, wouldn't it?

Jackie   I'm sure he is just thinking he doesn't want to disturb you. If anything was wrong he would get in touch. Did you / ever have a birth debrief with your midwife?

Nina   /That would be the kind thing to do. Ben will be going to bed by now hopefully. And I'm not there. Isn't it odd? Isn't it amazing? All this stuff. I mean. I've been craving tonight. So excited. I've absolutely loathed huge swathes of the last three months and all I've wanted is to be on my own. And now that I am I can't stop aching for him. I ache. Isn't it powerful? This soft torture. Because as soon as he arrived my relief at it all disappeared and was replaced with something else. This dawning. This creeping blood loss, pale face, dry mouth dread. Oh the things that could happen to him. The dreadful, awful things that could hurt or kill him. The things I must protect him from at all times. Every second must be taken up with this. And I don't know if it's the tiredness or hormones or maybe I'm going a little bit mad but sometimes I have found myself almost wishing . . .

She stops talking. Unable to speak. **Jackie** *waits.*

Nina *snaps out of it.*

Nina   Because here I am in the middle of it all and actually it feels a bit like I'm in quicksand. I'm in the sea. I'm in a, I'm in a, I'm in a. I don't know who I am anymore. Does that happen? Do you suddenly lose yourself with all this? I know I've heard mums talk about it but I thought it was just kind of 'Oh I can't keep on top of my moisturising routine anymore'. Not actual loss. Of self. Not actual who the fuck am I? I mean I know my name. I know I'm Nina. But other than that. I don't trust what I'm going to do. Am I mad now?

Jackie   I don't think you're mad. I think you're incredibly tired. And I think you've had a couple of drinks and you're unravelling. And that's a good thing.

Nina   I would do anything for him. I would. I'm sorry. I'm no fun anymore.

Jackie   Don't apologise. It's just nice to be with you.

Nina   I've missed you.

Jackie   Me too. But it's OK. You're right in the middle of the storm. Let go of the sails for a bit.

Nina   Mum used to say that too.

Nina *has got her phone in her hand and is staring at it.*

Jackie   Ni?

Nina *answers the phone.*

Nina   Hello?

She listens.

Nina   What kind of fit? Which hospital? I'm coming.

She hangs up the phone. **Jackie** *has already sprung to action.*

Jackie   You can't drive I'll get a taxi.

Nina   No, it'll take too long. He shouldn't have taken him.

Jackie   You can't drive, Nina.

Nina   I don't fucking care. He shouldn't have been away from me. This is my fault.

Jackie   Nina, it's OK. He'll be OK. Babies fit all the time.

Nina   Are you coming or not?

Jackie   Fuck.

They are now at a hospital.

Nina *alone again. Arms outstretched towards the door.*

Pearl *bursts in.*

Pearl   They've taken him in, Nina. He's being questioned right now.

Nina   What?

Pearl   They think the fit was because David did something which you know isn't true. So you go down there and you tell them that.

Nina   Where is Ben?

Pearl   You tell them David didn't do anything.

Nina   Where is Ben, Pearl?

Pearl   Come with me, Nina.

Nina   I will scream, so help me god, just tell me where my boy is!

Jackie *enters.*

Jackie   What's going on?

Nina   No one will tell me where Ben is.

Jackie   He's fine. He's safe. You'll see him soon.

Nina   I need to see him now.

Jackie   Nina, I promise you, he's fine. Pearl, what's wrong?

Pearl   They've taken David into some basement room to talk to him about Ben. They're saying he hurt him. It's barbaric.

Jackie   OK, calm down.

Pearl   I will not. My son would not do that. My son is not like that.

Jackie   You're overreacting, Pearl. I doubt they're interrogating him. It's part of their child protection policy. It's protocol. They need to make sure there's nothing else to it. They'll probably want to talk to Nina too.

Nina   Will they?

Jackie   Maybe. If they think the fit was linked to something else. They'll want to talk to you too, Pearl.

Pearl   Why me? I've done nothing either. This is harassment! David is a good father. Please, Nina. Come with me.

Jackie   Pearl, she's going nowhere. She needs to rest so she can look after Ben once he's discharged.

Pearl   Why aren't you with him now?

Jackie   She's been asked to stay here while they run some tests. You need to calm down.

Nina   What happened?

Pearl   You know what happened. Nothing did. The kid had a fit. I don't know, some kind of virus, it happens. He went up to check on Ben and he was fitting. So he was being a parent? He was being a responsible parent who checks on his child? What the hell else do you imagine he was doing?

Nina   Pearl, I don't know what's going on.

Pearl   You're his wife, Nina. He needs you. He needs you to go down there and tell them that he is a good dad and a good husband and that they should let him go.

Nina *doesn't respond. There is an uncomfortable pause.*

Pearl   Sorry. Sorry. This is too much. Sorry. Are you OK? This must be terrifying for you. I'm so sorry, Nina. I don't know what happened it was all so quick. Poor David was in such a panic. I was. We had no idea what was going on. It's all so strange. We put him to bed and next thing we know, we check on him and he's fitting. That's it. A virus they think. It's just a virus. I'm so sorry, love. Come here.

She hugs **Nina** *who barely responds.*

Pearl   I'm just scared for David and I wasn't thinking. And if you just came with me to vouch for him. I think that would help is all.

Jackie   They have procedures. I'm sure they'll call Nina soon.

Pearl   It's all so clinical.

Jackie   They need to be careful.

Pearl   Do you know how terrifying it was? Seeing Ben like that? No one should see their kid in that state. David was very upset. I'm very upset. If you'd been there/

Nina   What?

Pearl   If you'd been there with Ben you'd understand why I'm so flustered.

Nina   If I hadn't had a night off you mean?

Jackie   Right, time to go now, Pearl, I think.

Pearl   No, I don't mean it like that, for godsake.

Nina   It was David who suggested the night away at yours.

Pearl   I know.

Nina   I didn't want it to happen.

Pearl   Didn't you?

Nina   No.

Pearl   Why?

Nina   He's only three months old.

Pearl   Oh for godsake!

Nina   He's too small. I kept saying this but David and you kept pushing me.

Pearl   Encouraging you! Mothers need breaks!

Nina   Not after twelve weeks!

Pearl   David was staying with my parents after his first week.

Nina   That was your choice.

Pearl   After the birth you had you deserve time off.

Nina   I felt pushed into it.

Pearl   Ah well, a lot of things are done differently these days it seems. What do I know? I'm sure it's all for the better. Fathers are so much more included these days. No way David's father would have set foot in the labour ward. He popped by once it was all done and dusted and did I get any help from him after? Of course not. I doubt he changed a single nappy if I remember correctly. But it was fine because that was what I wanted to do and he was working long hours. That was normal then. It wasn't looked down on like it is now. I mean, the pressure on fathers to be the perfect parent and go out and earn the money really is such a burden these days. Not to say mothering isn't hard but it's in our nature isn't it? Men, god bless them, try as they might, they just don't have those natural abilities. Nothing against women who want to work but I was desperate to stay at home. No way I wanted to work. I loved being a mother to David and his brothers. That was my calling. And I don't care what people say, it's not as hard as going out every day to an office. It's hard but not *as* hard. These right-on types who try to make out like mothers have the short straw. What's so bad about being able to stay at home every day and do what you want? I loved it. Each to their own and all that, I know not everyone is the same but I simply don't understand these mothers who find it so hard.

Nina   I actually can't listen to this anymore. Jackie, take me to Ben.

Jackie   I can't, not yet.

Nina (*rounding on* **Pearl**)   Do you believe all that then?

Pearl   Sorry?

Nina   Is that something you actually believe or have you said it so many times now you don't know what else you would say?

Pearl   I don't know what you mean.

Nina   Your monologues.

Pearl   What is she talking about?

Jackie   Perhaps you should just leave her be.

Nina   You're good at speeches. And you never seem aware that you've done them before. I've heard that one so many times now I could probably do them myself.

Pearl   I'm just saying/

Nina   I know what you're saying. You're saying I'm a shit mum and David shouldn't be expected to do so much.

Pearl   No.

Nina   Yes you are. But you won't admit it. You're also saying that if I were to just do things your way then everything would be fine. You're good at conducting these speeches. You talk and talk and talk and all your men around you just let you. Filling gaps. Silences. Making sure no one actually says something they mean.

Pearl   You've been drinking, Nina. In the morning you may feel differently.

Nina   Maybe.

Pearl   Perhaps I should go and leave you to sleep it off.

Nina   No, you're here now so let's talk. How did mothering that child of yours turn out for you, then? You happy? In yourself?

Pause.

Nina   You a generally happy person, are you?

Pearl   Yes.

Nina   No you're not.

Pearl   That's not for you to say.

Nina   I've found every second of these months hard. Even the beautiful ones. Even the sleeping ones. And do you know what's made it harder? Your son.

Pearl   Now stop.

Nina   You were the one who barged in here wanting to talk.

Pearl   I wanted you to come down and get David out, actually.

Nina   Well, I won't do that because he should be in there.

Pearl   You don't mean that.

Nina   I do. Let me tell you something about your David. This is the guy who didn't know how to use an iron or a washing machine when I met him. He couldn't cook. He was living in a flat that was spotless but that's because you would come round once a week and clean it for him. He would either eat out or at yours or get take away. He didn't buy clothes because he always had plenty from you. He would talk to you every day. Sometimes several times a day. If I asked him when he was free he would consult with you. He didn't have a diary he had you. Keeping everything he needed in your mind. You booked his dental appointments. His doctor's check ups. His hair cuts. You did it all for him. He was twenty-six. He was twenty-six years old. I should have run for my fucking life.

Pearl   He's a good boy.

Nina   No he's not. I'll tell you some more about him you didn't know. Fucking loves porn.

Pearl   Oh now.

Nina   Loves it. More than anything sometimes. He tells me he doesn't watch it anymore but I know he does because he's shit at covering his tracks. His computer history is littered with sites. Likes them young.

Pearl   I'm going.

Nina   It's OK. I'm sure you are fairly savvy about it having raised three boys. Can't police it all. And anyway, what he likes to watch online has nothing to do with what it is that's scaring the crap out of you right now.

They stare at each other.

Is he capable of hurting his own child?

They stare.

Because I know you're only trying to protect your son. But I'm trying to protect mine.

Pearl   He wouldn't.

Nina   Wouldn't he?

Pearl   No.

Nina   A mother will do anything to protect her son.

Pearl   No.

Nina   How are we to protect them? Even from themselves? How are we to keep them alive? Safe? The weight of it. What if we get it wrong? Like those monsters on the news. Those women staring out at us who don't deserve to be called mother. Weren't they just like us at some point? Even for a split second? Hoping? Loving? Gently caring and trying. Trying so hard not to fuck it up?

Jackie   Is there something you need us to know, Nina?

Nina   No. What?

She looks at **Jackie** *who doesn't answer.*

Nina   Jackie? What do you mean?

Nina *suddenly looks away from* **Jackie** *at nothing.*

Jackie   Nina?

Nina   He's happy.

Pearl   What's wrong with her?

Nina *snaps out of it.*

Pearl   David is still downstairs and I won't leave him a moment longer. Will you come with me?

Nina   No.

Pearl   Please.

Nina   The problem with having control over everything is that when things go wrong everyone looks at you.

Pearl   What do you mean?

Nina   Well, David wasn't the only one there last night, was he?

Jackie   I think I should step in here.

Nina   No Jacks, you're alright.

Jackie   Nina, babies have fits.

Nina   No, it's not just that. They're questioning him because they're worried. They wouldn't question him for a virus. They told me they found a bruise. On Ben's ear. One I hadn't seen before so it must be new. They keep an eye out for bruises in unusual places. They said to me they wanted to do X-rays.

Pearl   What are you saying?

Nina   I'm saying go back to your son and tell him I'm not coming.

Pearl   What?

Nina   This is for you.

Pearl   What are you talking about?

Nina   Bit of me-time, eh?

Suddenly **Nina** *throws her arms up towards the door.* **Pearl** *and* **Jackie** *disappear.*

A shift. Time passes.

Nina *looks down and realises her breasts are leaking milk.*

Nina   Mum? Jackie?

No response. **Pearl** *enters.*

Nina   Is Jackie outside? I need some help?

Pearl   They're going to want to talk to you.

Nina   Pearl, can you find Jackie for me? I need her to get me a pump. Or I need to go to Ben.

Pearl   You won't be able to go to Ben.

Nina   What?

Pearl   They won't let you.

Nina   Is he OK? Oh god, what's happened?

Pearl   You tell me.

Nina   What are you talking about? Let me pass.

Pearl No. They're on their way up. I told them to come find you here.

Nina Who? I want to go to Ben.

Pearl You can't.

Jackie *bursts in.*

Nina Jackie, what's going on?

Pearl You were so cruel about my son. And it was you.

Jackie Pearl, get out. Nina, sit down.

Nina What is she talking about? I need to see Ben; look at me.

Jackie Listen to me. They want to talk to you. They did X-rays. Ben has fractures. On his skull and his ribs. There's bruising on his body too.

Pearl You're sick.

Nina What?

Jackie They're old injuries.

Pearl You said it was David and it wasn't.

Jackie Pearl, get the fuck out.

Nina I didn't do anything to him though.

Jackie They still want to talk with you. There can be other explanations for these kinds of things.

Nina They won't let me see him?

Jackie They can't. Not until they've established what's going on.

Nina Oh god, I'd never hurt him. This is wrong.

Jackie Just wait here, OK? Just wait. Pearl, go away.

Pearl I knew it. I knew it about you.

Jackie Pearl, this isn't helping and you know nothing. If anything David is still in trouble too.

Pearl   He's not the one looking after him all the time.

Jackie   You look after him every week. Is it you we should be looking at?

Pearl   Don't be ridiculous.

Jackie   Well then. Fuck off and leave us alone.

Pearl   So righteous, Nina. Always so righteous.

She leaves.

Nina   Jackie, what am I going to do?

Jackie   Don't panic yet. They're doing blood tests. There's a chance he has some kind of problem which would involve fractures.

Nina   I didn't do anything to him.

Jackie   And David?

Nina   I don't know. Maybe? I would have noticed, wouldn't I?

Jackie   I don't know.

Nina   And Pearl has him one morning a week. Oh Ben! Oh god! My boy! My boy!

She begins to shake uncontrollably.

Nina   I need to feed him. I'm leaking. I need to feed him.

Jackie   I'll find you a pump.

Nina   No, I want to feed him. I need him.

Jackie   You can't.

Nina   Who has him?

Jackie   He's still with the nurses. Let me speak to them about it. You might be able to feed under supervision.

Nina   Will I be arrested?

Jackie   You might.

Nina   Pearl said they were coming up to get me.

Jackie   They will probably want to discuss things with you and ask you to come down to the station voluntarily.

Nina   I have to feed before then. I have to.

Jackie   Let me see what I can do.

Nina   What if they come to get me before you get back?

Jackie   I'll be quick.

Nina   Please Jackie, I need him.

Jackie   I know.

She leaves.

Nina *is rocked by what could be a storm or a great wind or electric shock.*

Nina   What happens now? What happens now? What happens now?

Pearl *is there but it's not* **Pearl**.

Nina   Eight.

Pearl   Wait.

Nina   Mum?

Pearl   You're going to have to wait.

Nina   Yes. It'll be lovely for everyone.

Pearl   Are you sure?

Nina   What?

Pearl   About him? Are you?

Nina   Don't start this please.

Pearl   I just don't like the vibe he gives off.

Nina   This is so unhelpful.

Pearl   I wouldn't forgive myself if I didn't say something.

Nina   I love him, Mum.

Pearl   I know.

Nina   I really love him.

Pearl   And it's clouding your judgement.

Nina   I don't know what you've got against him.

Pearl   I don't trust him. When I'm gone. I need you to be OK.

Nina   Stop it.

Pearl   I don't trust him one bit.

Nina   Mum, you're getting yourself worked up.

Pearl   I'm only looking out for my child. That's all. I'm protecting my child.

Nina   Sorry?

Jackie *is there but it's not* **Jackie**. **Nina** *is in a police interview room.*

Jackie   I'll repeat the question. Did you at any point hit baby Ben?

Nina   No.

Jackie   Did you drop him or shake him?

Nina   No.

Jackie   Did you intentionally slap him?

Nina   No.

Jackie   Perhaps in a moment of anger? Did you throw him heavily to the floor?

Nina   No.

Jackie   Did you kick him or punch him?

Nina   No.

Jackie   Did you try to snap his arm bone?

Nina   No!

Jackie   Did you squeeze him too hard?

Nina   No.

Jackie   Did you push him?

Nina   No.

Jackie   Did you get so tired and so frustrated with his crying that you harmed him?

Nina   (*suddenly angry*)   No. No. I won't have this. He is my child. He is mine and I have done nothing to harm him and this is all so wrong. What is happening? I won't have this. Let me see him. Let me fucking see him. Let me fucking see him. LET ME FUCKING SEE HIM.

There is a tussle between her and **Jackie** *as she tries to leave the room. When she is shoved back in it has become her Mum's house.* **Pearl** *isn't* **Pearl**. *This is the past.*

Pearl   Why are you bringing this up now?

Nina   Because my therapist suggested it might help me if I understood things from your perspective.

Pearl   Fucking bullshit.

Nina   I'll leave if you do your usual.

Pearl   No. I just don't get it. You know I don't get it.

Nina   I know but it's helping, so.

Pearl   Well what then?

Nina   The stuff I keep getting stuck on is when I was little.

Pearl   Look, it was very different. It was very hard. I was on my own.

Nina   This isn't about me blaming you for anything.

Pearl   It feels it.

Nina   No, it isn't. I'm trying to make sense of stuff in my head. Memories. I just need your view.

Pearl   I found it very hard is my view. And you're alive, aren't you?

Nina   I know. I just. I have this loop going in my head where you're driving away from me and I don't know whether that was school or when I stayed with Aunty Ellen. Or just dropping me at a friends. But it loops.

Pearl   I don't know.

Nina   And night times. Did you used to go out? When I was in bed?

Pearl   Possibly. I can't remember.

Nina   I was on my own at night a lot.

Pearl   You were fine.

Nina   OK.

Pearl   I was never one of those kinds of mothers.

Nina   What do you mean?

Pearl   It didn't come naturally to me. I don't mind admitting it. I don't recommend it.

Nina   What?

Pearl   Motherhood. It's not something we do well in our family.

Nina   I think you did your best and like you said, I'm alive.

Pearl   By the skin of your fucking teeth.

Nina   I'm going to move out, Mum.

Pearl   What?

Nina   David's found a place for us.

Pearl *looks at her and turns and walks away.*

Nina   Mum?

Nina *is back in her house. It is no longer the past.* **Jackie** *is* **Jackie** *again.* **Nina** *is using a breast pump.*

Jackie   Just me.

Nina *doesn't respond.*

Jackie   I brought a few things for the fridge. Milk, eggs, bread. Some fruit. I'm guessing you've not had much time to shop. We should get the heat on and warm the place up. Tea?

No response. **Jackie** *goes off to unpack the shopping and put the kettle on. She comes back.*

Jackie   Welcome home.

Nina   Yes.

Jackie   I came over yesterday and tidied up some stuff. I think when David came to get his things he did it in a hurry. I'm not sure he's taken everything. I put a bag of his clothes in the garage for you to deal with when you're ready.

Nina   Thank you.

Jackie   It was a real mess.

Nina   Thank you.

Jackie   You got a court date yet?

Nina   No. The cancelled one was rescheduled and then that one got cancelled too, I don't know why. Waiting.

Jackie   I bet it was good getting out of your mum's.

Nina   I wanted to be there.

Jackie   I know.

Nina   I chose to be there.

Jackie   Why?

Nina   Cos it was Mum's.

Jackie   It's in a nice spot.

Nina   Most of her stuff has gone. It's pretty empty.

Jackie   I'm amazed it's not sold.

Nina   Took it off the market.

Jackie   I tried knocking a few times.

Nina   Six months.

Jackie   I left your bed alone. I couldn't find where you keep your clean sheets.

Nina   The last time I was here. Was.

Jackie *waits for her to finish but she doesn't.*

Jackie   The pizza boxes were still in the front garden.

Nina   Foxes.

Jackie   Yeh, probably.

Nina   Why does it need to take this long?

Jackie   You heard from David?

Nina   No.

Jackie   Pearl?

Nina   No. Jacks?

Jackie   Yeh?

Nina   You know who to speak to. I have a freezer full of my milk. They won't take it for him. I just want him to have it. Will you talk to someone for me? I don't know if they're passing my messages on.

Jackie   I'll try.

Nina *seems relieved.*

Nina   Thank you. And Jacks?

Jackie   Yes?

Nina   My solicitor said you will be asked to speak in court.

Jackie   Do you want to do this now?

Nina   Yeh.

Jackie   It's my job.

Nina   What will you tell them?

Jackie   I only told them what you told me.

Nina   What if they use it?

Jackie   What do you mean?

Nina   Some of the stuff I said to you.

Jackie   I can't lie.

Nina   What if they misunderstand it and I never see him again?

Jackie   The court has to act in his best interests.

Nina   I'm his best interest. I'm his mum.

Jackie   I know.

Nina   I'm his mum.

Jackie   I know.

Nina   This whole fucking thing has been one long nightmare. The accusations, the evidence, the interviews, the home visits. The off and on and off and on of court dates. The waiting. And no one at any time has said 'That child just needs his mum – give him back. That mum needs her child'.

Jackie   They have to make sure you aren't a danger to him.

Nina   I'M NOT. I'M NOT. I'M NOT.

Jackie   But they have to be sure.

Nina   And in the meantime we are separated? My boy and me are apart. While they decide. While they work it all out. Slowly. Ever so fucking slowly because of paperwork and procedure. And me and Ben are apart. All this time because of them. Neither of us did anything wrong and we are apart. That can't be right, can it?

Everyone always says that in whatever situation the child should always be with their mother. That it's very fucking rare for a child to be taken from their mother. A breastfeeding child. A baby. But no. Because of suspicion. Because of that nurse. Because of that doctor. Because of that social worker. Because of the evidence from her friend that said she had been contemplating hurting her boy. Because of betrayal. Because of words. Because of exhaustion and wine and unravelling. Because. Because. And all this time we are apart. And I need him. And he needs me. And now because of all that time it might be too late. It might be too late for him and me. And then that's it.

Jackie (*snapping*)　And what if it was too late for him? What if they give him back to you too soon and you're unable to cope? Or that actually you had been the one to harm him and they have simply given a baby back to their abuser? What if that is what happens? That is the decision they are having to make. It doesn't matter how fucking much you miss him. Or even how fucking much he misses you because actually. Actually. He is safer in a neutral environment. He is safer where they know that no one would be trying to harm him. And open your eyes, Nina, and look properly at yourself for one minute. Would you honestly say that you would give a baby back to you? Even if you absolutely definitely hadn't harmed him? Look at you. Look at how you've been through all of this. You're a fucking mess. You're a shell. You can barely look after yourself let alone a baby. And not only that but you wouldn't even entertain the idea that you needed help. That perhaps things had gone a bit too far. That maybe things were too hard for you. You couldn't even talk to me about your birth. Because that was the catalyst, wasn't it? That was where this started. Or was it your mum? Was it that? And did the birth just kind of solidify everything? Is this too much? Is all this too much now for you? What are you feeling? If you want this all to stop, engage with it properly and actually tell me what it is you're feeling.

Nina　I don't know.

Jackie　You fucking do. Tell me.

Nina   I don't know.

Jackie   Tell me.

Nina   Empty?

Jackie   Bullshit. Tell me.

Nina   Lost?

Jackie   No. Tell me.

Nina   Hurt?

Jackie   Pathetic.

Nina   Upset.

Jackie   No.

Nina   Angry.

Jackie   OK.

Nina   I'm angry.

Jackie   Why?

Nina   Because no one believes me.

Jackie   About what?

Nina   Ben. That I wouldn't harm him.

Jackie   Do you blame them?

Nina   No. Yes. No.

Jackie   And what?

Nina   That I couldn't do it. I couldn't physically do it.

Jackie   What?

Nina   Look after him. It was so hard. It was too hard.

Jackie   And that made you angry?

Nina   Yes. And no one asked me if I was OK. After he came. Like
he arrived and I'd just been through. Been through. Something. So

hard. So. Too much. And no one actually really asked me if I was OK. Not in a way that made me want to tell them. Safe enough to tell them. It was like that hadn't just happened and now I had to just get on with the job of looking after a baby but I was just like. Just. It was like I was standing there in the middle of a busy road and this huge car crash had just happened and it was horrible. A horrible mess. And everyone except me. Like everyone was just carrying on. Going to the shops. Driving their cars around it. They couldn't even see it. And I was the only one who could. And maybe I should have shouted out something to alert people to it but I didn't because maybe the car crash hadn't happened or at least wasn't as bad as I had thought it was and that I should just ignore it and get on with things. Other people seemed so much more capable of coping with the car crash than me. I needed to suck it up but I wish I'd shouted. Actually. Yes. What if I had shouted?

Jackie   What if you had shouted.

Nina   But I didn't.

Jackie   No.

Nina   When he was born I was so exhausted and brutalised I couldn't look at him. I didn't want to associate his tiny perfect face with that feeling. I couldn't. And I was so angry. With myself. For that. I felt weak and empty and how would I be enough for him? Protect him?

Jackie   This.

Nina   But.

Jackie   This is it.

Nina   But none of this meant I hurt him.

Jackie   . . .

Nina   Did it?

Jackie *goes.* **Pearl** *is there.*

Pearl   Would you like a bath?

Nina Sorry?

Pearl You look like you haven't washed in a few days. Let's sort you out.

Nina No.

Pearl What did you have for breakfast?

Nina Sorry?

Pearl Have you had anything?

Nina It's just I could do with being alone, Pearl. I really appreciate you coming but I just need to be on my own for a bit.

Pearl I know, love. But you have been for a while now and I think David is worried. Are you planning to come home soon? This place is so cold.

Nina It's fine.

Pearl You're coming up to the final weeks now you should be looking after yourself. And that bump of yours. Let us take the load with sorting out this place. Your mum wouldn't have wanted you to over exert yourself for her. Let us get it on the market for you. I can do a clean up, make it look nice for the photos.

Nina NO! No. Sorry. No. Leave it. Leave everything as it is. Leave it. Please.

Pearl OK.

Nina I just need space.

Pearl OK.

Nina I'm fine. Tell David I'll be home on the weekend.

Pearl I will.

Nina Tell him I'm fine.

Pearl . . .

Nina Tell him I'll be fine.

They are now in court.

Nina *stands in a stiff and nervous way. She is speaking to* **Jackie** *who both is and isn't* **Jackie**.

Jackie   Your mum died just before Ben arrived, is that correct?

Nina   Yes. But I don't see how that would have any bearing on all this.

Jackie   Just answer the question.

Nina   OK. But. OK fine. Yes, my mum died a month before Ben arrived . . . cancer. Well. Dementia too but it was the cancer really. That took her. Anyway she'd had dementia for a while and I'd been caring for her a lot up 'til about three months before she died and then we got some funding for some twenty-four-hour care and they kind of took over and Mum didn't need me there all the time and then actually she didn't want me there so for the last month it was just the carers and they would keep me posted with it all. They were nice enough. I was grateful. For them. And then it was hospital and she went pretty quick. A week in all. I wasn't there. She didn't want a fuss. Sorry. Is this what you meant? I'll stop.

Jackie   And you were the only person in her life?

Nina   Yes. Just me.

Jackie   So you had no help from family when things became difficult for her? That must have been hard. The obligation to help her even when you were struggling.

Nina   Yes, I guess. But it's what you do, isn't it?

Jackie   And these feelings of obligation – would you say you have similar when it comes to caring for your son?

Nina   Yes, but it's different, isn't it? Ben is my boy. I look after him because that's my job. As his mum.

Jackie   But it's hard, isn't it? Sometimes so hard you don't feel like you can cope. Particularly with your history of anxiety. Perhaps it was so hard it makes you feel swamped and frustrated and even angry?

Nina   He's my little boy.

She breathes a bit heavily suddenly.

Jackie   Are you OK? Would you like to take a short break?

Nina   No, I'm OK. Look, when Mum went it was sad, of course, but it was a relief. I don't want you making out like it affected me like, I don't know, like most normal people. Not that I'm not normal. I'm normal. I mean. Fuck. Look, I'm saying that Mum needed to die because she was so ill for so long and she was miserable. I mean she was miserable all her life. Since me, she said. And actually I get it. I get it now.

Jackie   So would you say you became depressed since the birth of your own child?

Nina   What?

Jackie   You say you 'get it'. That you get that she was depressed. That you have experienced the same.

Nina   No! Well, yes, she was depressed. She was a depressive. I lived with that, I know what that's like. I didn't ever want that for Ben. No, no, no I won't have you say that. I'm not like her. I'm not like that. Why haven't you asked me about David yet? Ask me about David. Ask me about him.

Jackie   Nothing further.

Nina   Ask me about him!

Jackie   Nothing further.

Nina   Mum?

Jackie   Nothing further.

Nina   Mum?

Nina *is back at her mum's house.* **Pearl** *is there but both is and isn't* **Pearl***.*

Pearl   One day you'll fucking get it.

Nina   You keep saying.

Pearl   One day you'll understand. When you have your own. It's not my fault.

Nina   OK, Mum.

Pearl   You won't be so angry with me then.

Nina   You need to rest.

Pearl   Why don't you come round anymore?

Nina   I'm here now, aren't I?

Pearl   You've not been all week.

Nina   I've had work.

Pearl   I don't like her.

Nina   Who?

Pearl   That cunt.

Nina   Don't. We need her. You need her.

Pearl   You do. Without her you'd have to do it all. You'd have to pull your finger out.

Nina   I can't, I have work.

Pearl   We could spend the money we spend on her on you instead. You could move back in. I'm no bother.

Nina   We wouldn't get the same money if it's me. And anyway, you don't want me wiping your arse. You'd fucking hate that.

Pearl   Why? Aren't you very good at it?

Nina   No I mean/

Pearl   /I know what you mean. You don't want to be wiping your own mother's arse.

Nina   Well. No.

Pearl   I've wiped yours enough times over the years.

Nina   Look, can we not? I would be no good at it. I want you properly cared for.

Pearl   Of course you'd be good at it!

Nina   I wouldn't. I'm too selfish. I'd get pissed off with you. I want to just be able to enjoy being with you.

Pearl   Ach fine.

Nina   I'll come round more.

Pearl   No you won't.

Nina   I will. Mum. Me and David.

Pearl   Oh that fuck.

Nina   We.

Pearl   Nice of him to visit, eh?

Nina   I know. I'm sorry.

Pearl   Nice of him to fucking visit.

Nina   Mum.

Pearl   You getting a divorce then?

Nina   What? No.

Pearl   What is it? You killed him? I wouldn't blame you.

Nina   No, Mum. I'm pregnant.

No answer.

Nina   Mum?

Pearl   Get rid of it.

Nina   What?

Pearl   It's not a good idea.

Nina   I can't!

Pearl   Selfish.

Nina   What?

Pearl   You. You're too selfish. Get rid of it. Get that fucking thing out of you. It's not worth it. None of this is worth it. Look at me. Look at me. Don't do it. Don't do it. Don't do it.

We're back in the courtroom. **Jackie** *and* **Pearl** *both are and aren't* **Jackie** *and* **Pearl**. **Nina** *watches.*

Jackie   'I get why people shake their babies.'

Pearl   You are saying that her exact words were 'I get why people shake their babies'.

Jackie   Yes.

Pearl   And did she confide any further in you about these urges?

Nina *both is and isn't* **Nina**.

Nina   Objection! Leading! What urges? Sustained! Please reword your question!

Pearl   OK. Did she confide any further about such thoughts.

Jackie   She did.

Nina   Objection! This is new information, we haven't seen this.

Pearl   Witness statement taken on the fifth of this month.

Nina   What?

Pearl   Please continue.

Jackie   She was very angry. I was concerned by how quickly she jumped from thought to thought.

Nina   Objection! Not a psychologist!

Jackie   She was almost frantic. She clearly had not slept much which isn't surprising considering she has a young baby but it was affecting her more than other mothers I've worked with.

Nina   Objection! Conjecture!

Pearl   Would you say that she was capable of harming her baby?

Jackie   I obviously can't say what had been happening in the weeks before but from her behaviour I would suggest that it's not outside the realms of possibility.

Pearl   Not outside the realms of possibility. Thank you.

Nina   They're just thoughts.

Pearl   Order!

Nina *ignores her and continues, determined to be heard.*

Nina   I don't act on them.

Pearl   I shall hold you in contempt!

Nina   It's only ever thoughts.

Pearl   Order! For godsake!

Nina   Look, I said all that to Jackie because she's my friend. People say stuff to friends. In fucking. In fucking. In fucking confidence. Yeh? I didn't mean it. It was just me. I was unravelling. She said it. I was tired. I am tired. She knows it. Didn't she tell you that? Didn't she? I would never. I would never. Please! Get him back to me.

Jackie *both is and isn't* **Jackie.**

Jackie   Can we take it back to the birth for a moment?

Nina   Why?

Jackie   You've spoken about your depression since having a baby and since the death of your mother and now I want to examine how your birth has affected your mental health.

Nina   I've not said I was depressed.

Jackie   I have an assessment here that strongly suggests you were. Can you tell us about your birth?

Nina   No.

Jackie   Pardon?

Nina   No. It's nothing to do with any of this.

Jackie   It might be. That is for the court to decide.

Nina   I'm a good mother.

Jackie   Please answer the question.

Nina   I would never harm my child.

Jackie   What was Ben's birth like?

Nina   Like nothing and everything.

Jackie   Pardon?

Nina   Like snow and fire. Like the possibilities were too huge and too terrifying to even go on but somehow I did. Like a great flood. Like precious metals and rust and everything in between. Blood. And eyes. Looking at me but not saying anything. Held breaths. Fear so strong I could hold it. Here. In here. I held it in here. Why is this relevant? What are you trying to say? I almost lost him. Why would I try to harm him? Why would I try to harm him. WHY WOULD I TRY TO HARM HIM?

Something shifts.

Nina   I thought I would be able to do this. Maybe I can't.

Something shifts. **Jackie** *isn't* **Jackie**.

Jackie   How do you feel in yourself at the moment, Nina?

Nina   What?

Jackie   Like now. Right now. How do you feel now? How do you think you might feel in an hour? How do you think you might feel tomorrow? Or the next? Because that's important now.

Nina   What is this?

Jackie   Because it's not just good enough to need him. To want him back. Your love will only go so far for all this. Because you will be on your own with him. And I need to know what that means to you. When he's crying again. And you have no one to help. How will that feel? How will you cope with that? Are you going to be able to ask for help?

Nina   'I need to know.' Are you assessing me?

Jackie   Are you going to get some help?

Nina   Is this you assessing me?

Jackie   Answer the questions please.

Nina   Fuck!

Jackie   I need to know on a scale of one to ten how you feel right now/

Nina   Scale!

Jackie   With one being suicidal and ten being ecstatically happy.

Nina   I'm a fucking. I'm a fucking hundred, is that what you want? I'm minus a hundred too. I'm everything! What the fuck? You're assessing me?

Jackie   They want my opinion.

Nina   Who do?

Jackie   The case team. Deciding on Ben. They called.

Nina   And what will you say?

Jackie   . . .

Nina   What will you say to them?

Jackie   That I don't think you are ready to have him back yet.

Nina   What?

Jackie   Because you're not.

Nina   Why?

Jackie   Because your behaviour is erratic. Because your version of events never made sense. Because you have made it clear to me in the past that you do not think you can be a good mum.

Nina   Oh god.

Jackie   Acknowledge what you did.

Nina   I didn't do anything!

Jackie   Regardless. He was hurt.

Nina   It wasn't me!

Jackie   But if you acknowledge that the reason this all happened was because you could not cope. And admit that you aren't ready to have him back yet. Then I will ask them to take this into account. This is all so time sensitive. I don't think you fully grasp how tricky this is.

Nina   I want him back!

Jackie   It's very simple. Take responsibility and ask for help.

Nina   This isn't real. This can't be real.

Jackie   I'm doing this for you.

Nina   I need him, Jackie! He needs me!

Jackie   I don't think he does.

Something shifts.

Pearl *isn't* **Pearl**.

Pearl   I don't want you to see me like this.

Nina   Mum, I've seen you in worse states.

Pearl   Please.

Nina   What am I supposed to do? Leave you to die alone?

Pearl   I have that woman.

Nina   You've got me! I'm here! Let me help you!

Pearl   It's never as simple as that though. Is it? We're all just trying to do our best but everyone has their own stuff going on and we need to get on with it.

Nina   No. No you're not well so I can care for you.

Pearl   And you?

Nina   I'm fine.

Pearl   When I'm gone.

Nina   Stop saying that.

Pearl   With the baby.

Nina   I'm fine, Mum.

Pearl   What if you're not?

Nina   Then don't go.

Pearl   What use would I be to you anyway.

Nina   Don't go.

Pearl   I fucked it all up.

Nina   You didn't.

Pearl   It's so hard, Nina. You'll see. I wasn't ready to be a mum.

Nina   But you were one. You were mine. And that's enough sometimes, isn't it?

Pearl   Have you told yourself that recently?

A shift.

Jackie   There are so many unknowns. Really, there's no knowing, is there? What happened. Or what could happen. And if you fixate on only the worst thing then what space do you leave yourself for enjoying the present?

Nina   There is no space.

Jackie   That's what I'm worried about.

Nina   If they take him then what would be the point?

Jackie   What do you mean?

Nina   I can't live without him. So they have to give him back.

Jackie   Nina.

Nina   It's OK, Jackie. I know they will give him back. They have to. I've done nothing wrong.

We're back in court. **Pearl** *isn't* **Pearl**.

Pearl   In the case of Baby Ben we are unable to reach a conclusive verdict. In the councel's representations we have found the evidence that this was a non-accidental injury to be lacking. The likelihood, based on the expert witnesses, testimonial and the evidence from family members, is that this child suffers from a rare condition that can mean that he is more susceptible to fracture and bruising. That any harm done to him by his parents or close relatives must have been unintended. It is this court's recommendation that Baby Ben will need careful monitoring from now on to make sure his condition is properly treated.

Nina   Is this it? Do I get him home?

Pearl   In recognition of the time this has taken to come to court we are also ruling on Ben's future guardianship. It has been brought to the attention of the court by Ben's case worker that as the process of this investigation has been longer than six months he has become settled with his foster family.

Nina   What?

Pearl   The family have begun proceedings to apply for adoption and it is the case worker's opinion that in the interest of Ben he should not be moved. I quote from her report 'Ben seems very happy and settled with his foster parents. He has fitted into their family very smoothly. They are also demonstrating great care in how they are coping with his condition and I am of the opinion that moving him now will further disrupt his development.'

Nina   No!

Pearl   It is with obvious regret that the proceedings took so long and perhaps if they had not then there could have been a different outcome but we must only work with the current situation. Therefore it is this court's recommendation that Baby Ben stays where he is in the interest of his own well being. The details will be passed down via the clerks. This concludes our hearing. Thank you.

Something impacts **Nina**. *Her panic intensifies.*

Jackie *both is and isn't* **Jackie**.

Jackie   Shh shh shhhh

Nina   Mum.

Pearl   Breathe. It's OK. You've been doing so well, Nina.

Nina   Have I?

Jackie   We're all so proud of you.

Nina   I miss you.

Pearl   Hush now. Shut your eyes.

Nina   I can't sleep.

Jackie   Shut your eyes.

Nina   You won't go?

Pearl   Let go of the sails, Nina.

Nina   OK.

Jackie   Let go.

Nina   OK.

Pearl   Shut your eyes then.

Nina   I can't.

Jackie   Shut your eyes.

Nina   I don't know what I'm supposed to do. Mum? What am I supposed to do?

Jackie   Deep breaths.

Nina   Mum, why wouldn't you let me help you? What if he thinks I left him? He needs me. Oh god help.

Pearl   Nina.

Nina   Mum? He needs me. I have to get him. I have to hold him. I have to show him I'll never leave him.

Jackie   Breathe.

Nina   Mum? I don't know what I'm doing. Help me! Mum?
Mum? Mum? I need you! Someone help me! Help me! HELP ME!

Jackie   One breath in, Nina, and one breath out. That's all it is.
Nina. That's all it is.

Something primal comes out of **Nina**. *She stands arms outstretched
towards the door.*

Nina *is frozen to the spot for a moment before the sound of a door
opening and closing makes her take notice.* **Pearl** *enters.*

Pearl   Sorry darlin', I checked the bag and realised I think I left
the new pack of dummies you gave me in the kitchen, I won't be a
mo.

She exits in a different direction. **Nina** *watches her go. After a
moment* **Pearl** *returns with dummies.*

Pearl   I'd forget my head if it weren't screwed on. You OK, love?

Nina *doesn't answer.*

Pearl   Oh look, he'll be fine. David's getting him in the car seat
right now and he's as happy as Larry. And like I said, if at any
point we think he needs to see his mum we'll bring him straight
back. But he won't. I want you to try and rest tonight, OK? This is
for you. You're exhausted and this is a well earned break. Will
Jackie be here soon?

Nina *looks confused but manages to answer.*

Nina   Eight.

Pearl   Well, why don't you run a bath. Bit of me-time eh? And
don't you fret, I'll be right there to help David. He has back up!
It'll be lovely for everyone. And we'll get him back to you in the
morning not too early. You've been doing so well Nina. We're all
so proud of you.

She gives **Nina** *a big hug.* **Nina** *sinks into it.*

Pearl   Your mum would be too. Rest up darlin'. You're too hard on yourself. He'll be back in your arms in no time.

Pearl *leaves.* **Nina** *stands arms outstretched from the hug towards the door.*

Suddenly **Pearl** *returns and goes straight to* **Nina** *and hugs her.*

Nina *exhales then sobs with a sharp intake of breath.*

The scene dissolves.

She is on the sea shore. The sound of the waves, womblike, surround her. She drops her bag. She takes a deep breath. She starts stripping off clothes to reveal her swimming costume. We leave her getting ready to submerge. Today, at least, everything is going to be alright.

End.

When the Long Trick's Over

Morgan Lloyd Malcolm

When the Long Trick's Over was originally co-produced by HighTide and New Wolsey Theatre. It had its first performance on 11 February 2022 at New Wolsey Theatre in Ipswich. The cast was as follows:

Swimmer   Stacey Ghent
Mum   Shenagh Govan

Creative Team

Writer: Morgan Lloyd Malcolm
Director: Chinonyerem Odimba
Designer: Grace Smart
Lighting and Video Designer: Gillian Tan
Sound Designer: Esther Kehinde Ajayi
Production Manager: David Phillips
Aerial and Movement Consultant: Vicki Dela Amedume
Associate Aerial Consultant: Graeme Clint
Assistant Director: Helena Snider
Artist Wellbeing Practitioner: Lou Platt
Company Stage Manager: Judith Volk
Technical Stage Manager: Shaun Barber
Costume Supervisor: Kira Tisbury

A large expanse of water. Whether this is a tank or the whole stage or whatever. Whether real or not. The presence and sense of water is important. Enough for someone to swim in or at least appear to swim in. Enough for someone to float or at least appear to float in a boat on. The play must be similarly fluid. Moments bleed into each other as they jump across the **Swimmer***'s consciousness. It's also important not to be scared to have pauses in dialogue while she swims. These moments of silence when all we hear is the sound of her swimming and the wind and sea are just as important as what she says. She has just started a swim across the English Channel. She starts in the night so it is dark at first.*

Swimmer The cold. The cold is the thing. Many people don't manage it because of the cold. Amazing swimmers. Strong swimmers. They just get too cold. It's actually one of those things where a bit of body fat comes in handy. Which is good for me. I don't see me having to pull myself up onto the boat half way there. Plenty of insulation. As Mum would say – I've got my blubber jacket on. Finally it has some use.

I mean I'm ready. I've done so many training swims. Cold water and me; we know each other. But there's always that bit when you first get in that you're like 'oh for fucksake what am I doing?' And I mean, that thought is like doubly so right now. Triply. Hundredly. Channel swim? Fucksake what am I doing?

Beautiful glowing lights all around us.

You see those lights? Those are glowsticks. That's my crew on the boat lighting my way. They know this is the bit I was dreading most. Night swimming is my worst. But those lights I can fix on. I can see they've got them hanging round their necks too because I can see them moving round the boat. Have you ever swum at night? It's mind over matter, that's what it is. Because it's pitch fucking black down there. I mean. Pitch. Like. I'm thinking stupid stuff right? Like Jaws right? Like I mean you know. You know. So I have strategies right?

This is what I do. Top ten nineties tunes. 10: 'Regulate' by Warren G. No. 10: 'Ebeneezer Goode' then 9: 'Regulate'. 8: Dub Be Good

To Me. 7: 'Killing Me Softly With His Song' or 'Fugee-La'. Fugees are my 1996 even if they were earlier than that. They were my GCSEs. They were the hot summer we had. They were going down to the river to spend ages working up to a swim because a swim meant getting into swimming gear in front of the boys. Hot summers spent in long trousers and baggy t-shirts because I was shit at shaving my legs. 6: 'Save Tonight'. 5: 'Mmm Bop'. 4: 'Together Again', Janet Jackson – it was about some friend of hers that died. I just loved the dance routine in the video. Tried to learn it but I mean, it's Janet Jackson and her choreographer was amazing. It's a really hard routine. 3: 'Crush'. Most people hate that song but I love it. No idea why. Probably because I wanted to be a secret pixie dream girl with lots of boyfriends without feeling unworthy and fat. 2: 'Closer than Close' by Rosie Gaines. There was a remix on the CD that was better than the single. Funkier. Loved that fucking song. Again, not many people would admit to it. 1: 'Don't Let Go', En Vogue. Mostly because of her. We would sing it together. Badly. In the car.

I once made Mum do it with me. From her hospital bed. She was pretty out of it on morphine and way more up for it than she normally would have been and she can't sing so it was pretty ridiculous but we had fun. Then she died. Maybe I need to stop making people sing En Vogue with me.

She swims.

I made these games when I was training. For the boredom mostly. But they, yeh, they help in other ways too. Because it's a really, really long way. It's 18.2 nautical miles which is approximately twenty-one land miles but that's if you are lucky. It can be longer. To finish in twelve hours is considered good. I will be lucky if I finish in under eighteen to be honest. I really hope it's not that long though. Obviously. But if it is then I have these games. I make lists. Top ten lists. It helps pass the time between feeds. Top ten nineties songs. Top ten animals I've ever known. Top ten times I've had a good night but ended up sad. Number one on that list was the night me and her went to Paris on the Eurostar but ended up in hospital with her pains again. Number seven was when I got so drunk I snogged a really, really hot footballer but then pissed myself on the dancefloor and so hid in the toilets instead of going home with him. Sad face.

Mum thought I was mad to even try this. They all did.

I memorised some poems too. Just to keep me going.

'I must go down to the seas again, to the lonely sea and the sky.'

That's John Masefield.

God it's dark down there. It's really really dark. I'm actually, hold up, I'm actually getting myself a bit, am I going the right way still? Hold up. Where's the . . .? Oh. Yeh. OK. Follow the light. Follow the light. Don't fixate. Fuck, too dark. Too dark. I hate this. I hate this. Swim.

She swims concentrated for a time. Just breath and darkness. Water and the sound of the boat engine. A voice from the boat is heard but is muffled; sounds encouraging.

We used to sit in my room, on my bed listening to our CDs together. I had a little portable CD player that I got one Christmas with the REM album and then most weekends we would have saved our pennies up so we could each buy a single. Or if we were lucky it was a birthday or we'd done a job round the house or something and we had a bit more cash and we would pool it and buy a whole album. Often it was hard to decide on one we both wanted so we would go for a compilation album like a NOW That's What I Call Music or somesuch. NOW 22 had 'Finally' by Cece Peniston on it and oh my god if we didn't play that a hundred times. I mean she was mostly just wanting to dance to it but I was thinking about Joey Fletcher who was in my class and had floppy curtain hair and wore his polo shirts baggy and looked a bit like he should be in an American boy band. All I wanted was for him to fancy the pants off me and ask me to go to the cinema so we could sit in the double seats at the back and snog but he liked Jo because Jo was cute and giggly and pretty and wouldn't it be funny if they went out because he was called Joey and she was called Jo and she was also my best friend but for fucksake Jo for fucksake. And she did ask me first if it was OK for them to start going out but. So the lyrics of 'Finally' were basically me because I was just waiting for things to happen to me in the way that they were supposed to. You know; get boyfriend, snog, be cool, rule the world. But I was more a best mate than a girlfriend. And now I look back on it I think I had a lucky escape actually. Because going out with boys back then basically seemed to involve letting them finger you in their bedrooms or behind bushes. I'm not sure it was the Hugh Grant/ Andie Macdowell love goal we wanted. Anyway my sister and I mostly shared the same taste for a short while but she was a few years younger than me and when Take That hit she was swept up in it all and I was like 'nah thanks, they're lame'. So while she was cutting out photos of Mark Owen and making heart shapes round them with ribbon and crying about how much she loved him I discovered Snoop Dogg's Dog Pound album and was making her play my casette in the car. I honestly thought when he rapped about doing it 'Doggy Style' was just Snoop being a bit braggy about how cool and stylish he was. It was Mum going apeshit at the lyrics that made me realise that sex was EVERYWHERE and I knew nothing about it and fuck I was uncool and I was going to die a virgin.

Somehow my sister never had all this. At least I didn't think she did at the time. I mean she was thin, and pretty and looked good in clothes. She didn't seem to care much what boys thought of her so it made boys love her more. She had a great laugh. She could make you think you were the best fucking person since Mark Owen. And for some weird stupid reason she looked up to me. Me. Stupid, fat, ugly, big foot, no boyfriend me. What was that all about? And even though she was amazing. Like really, really amazing – she really didn't think she was and oh my god it made me so angry. I used to tell her to 'get a fucking grip' and there was a lot of me telling her she should be grateful she could fit in a size 8 skirt. She hated upsetting me. I probably laid it on a bit thick. And then as she got older and her periods got worse it was less about how she looked and more about how she felt and fuck I wish I could have helped.

'And a grey mist on the sea's face, and a grey dawn breaking.'

I think I'm coming up to my first feed. That means I'm only an hour in.

A smallish whiteboard with the words 'One hour done, you're doing great!' written on it. A long pole with a little net on the end appears above her. She reaches in and brings out a jelly baby which she eats. A water bottle filled with an energy loading drink on a rope is thrown and lands near her in the water. She reaches for it and drinks. This all happens with speed. As soon as she's done the bottle and pole are pulled away and out of sight again.

I'm in a rhythm now. A lot of swimmers just focus on that. On their stroke. They don't think about anything other than getting to the next feed stop. Compartmentalise things. Something I'm usually really good at. Keeping things in their proper place. Not over analysing. But your mind can play tricks on you. Particularly when you're repeating the same thing over and over again. Arm over head. Elbows. Stretch. Pull.

She swims.

Fifth of July 1999. Heart break. I really didn't like myself very much in that moment. Cos everything was confirmed. All my worries. My first love and they no longer wanted me. In my head it was for all the reasons why no one wanted me before. I drove home from Birmingham of all places. One hundred miles or thereabouts. Crying and listening to R&B. Singing and crying. 'Scrying'? In my own personal music video. I probably should have crashed that night. I'm amazed actually. Motorway driving when scrying should probably not end well. And when I got home and threw myself into my sister's arms I remember her saying to me; 'please don't ever let anyone make you feel like this again'. And I haven't. Not really. Not since then. They've come and gone. But no one real. Which I'm not actually convinced is a good thing. But she made me believe that it was. But it's not about all that actually. What is it about?

I remember my sister watched all this with her own version of life going on in her head. And she told me later that she learnt something about love that day from me. That it was dramatic. That it hurt. That it made you feel so intensely you somehow lose great chunks of yourself. She described me that day as looking like a blur.

It's still so dark. I keep expecting something to just grab me.

I'm doing this for her because this was her dream. This isn't my natural habitat. I wouldn't normally choose this. But she would have. And I kind of felt like I had to do it. I feel like she wanted me to. Which isn't right now making it any easier. I can feel the urge to panic is, like, always right there. At the back of my eyeballs. At the back of my throat.

I wish the sun would come up.

It wasn't that she didn't care what others felt – she just didn't show it. Where I would scream and cry about my hurts she would disappear to her room. Reading or listening to music. I'd knock on the door and ask if she was OK. 'Fine' she'd say. Fine. That was before the pains started though.

Suddenly the overwhelming and startling sound of a large oil tanker's fog horn.

Shit shit shit!

She treads water. It is clear that she is very worried. She can't see very well. Shouts come from the boat to stay put. Lights move over the water. The light of her support boat focuses on her. She waits as the oil tanker goes by.

Usually they're supposed to avoid us, change course. Sometimes they can't. Just wait for the wash.

The wash of the oil tanker hits her and she is buffeted about. It's quite a bit impact. She struggles to stay calm. In waves she sees something. She can't quite make out what it is. It seems to be a rowing boat with a woman in it. It disappears.

What? Hello?

She continues to deal with the waves.

Fuck! Am I still pointed the right way? Where's my boat? There. OK. Hey!

She waves.

Am I OK to keep going? Do I keep swimming now? That felt very close.

She tries to hear a response.

I'll keep going!

She swims.

Suddenly feeling quite small.

Nineties list. Do the 90s list again. Yeh. So. The thing is about 90s stuff and in particular the R&B stuff was they were so overly dramatic. Stressy. Intense. Over explain-y. I loved it.

She sings – En Vogue 'Don't Let Go' with no backing.

Mum *appears as if summoned. She floats on in a rowing boat. Nothing too fancy. They really go for it with the singing. Still no backing track. Totally a capella.*

Mum (*interrupting, singing*)   'Hold me tight . . .'

Over the previous chorus **Mum** *has been heading off stage and by the final 'don't let go' she's gone. The song stops as soon as she's left.* **Swimmer** *looks off in the direction that she went for a moment then looks back out to sea.*

She waits a moment to see if **Mum** *returns.*

Swimmer   Not sure. If. Not sure if that would be something I need right now actually. Is she . . . (gone)?

Satisfied she's gone she carries on. She swims hard for a bit.

OK. So. When I was about nine I got caught in a rip. The thing is about those bastards is that they trick you. You don't realise how strong they are and you think you can swim against them to get back in because it was only moments before that you were close to shore. But they sweep you out so quick and no amount of swimming against them will help reverse that and all it will do is exhaust you. I was saved by a strong swimmer who came and pulled me into shore. What you do is you swim across a rip.

You might end up further down the beach but at least you are on land.

Mum *is suddenly there again.*

Mum   I had taught you this.

Swimmer   No fuck off.

Mum   I had. I know it's a better story if you say you learnt by being out there in the middle of it but actually I had told you. I'd taught you about this. You must always respect the sea.

Swimmer (*ignoring her*)   The worst bit was /

Mum   It will chew you up, the sea. It doesn't respect you.

Swimmer   / the offshore wind because I could hear Mum shouting for me but she couldn't hear me. I was shouting that I was coming, that I was OK but she couldn't hear and I knew she thought I was shouting for help and I couldn't bear that she was panicking when I felt like I was OK.

Mum   I wasn't panicking actually. Better drowned than duffers.

Swimmer   And then when I realised I wasn't OK and I was getting tired and so that's when I started to panic. The swimmer got to me before I went under.

Mum   If not duffers, won't drown. Swallows and Amazons.

Swimmer   That night, once home, I tried sleeping but all I could hear were waves. Like an echo. A deafening sound of crashing waves. And my mum shouting for me. Ever since then I've been scared of the sea. I know its power. It took me a while but I still wanted to get in it.

Mum   The good thing about the channel crossing is that you don't need to worry about rips.

Swimmer   OK. What the fuck are you doing here?

Mum   I'm interrupting your flow. I'll shush.

Swimmer   But why are you even here?

Mum   I'll just sit quietly. You won't even notice me.

Swimmer   I don't need you here, Mum. In fact it will be a massive fucking problem if you are here. So you can't be here. You're not here.

Mum   I'm not.

Swimmer   No, so fuck off.

She waits for **Mum** *to disappear.* **Mum** *just sits in her boat trying to be discreet.* **Swimmer** *decides to ignore her and continue swimming.*

Summer (*urgently*)   She gave me all the links. All the info. She told me to meet up with some others who had made the crossing already. She told me how to do the training. She gave me a schedule. How to book my slot on one of the boats. She was the one who said I needed to book for a couple of years' time and that way I would get the first slot on any particular date as if I got the second or third I would stand more chance of it being postponed due to weather. They will always try to get the first slot across first and if the weather is being kind the other slots follow. She told me all this because she had been researching it herself for her own crossing. She was supposed to be doing it. It was a lifelong dream really. She'd always said she wanted to do it. But I think she knew she wouldn't.

Mum   Just one of many things she failed to do.

Swimmer   NO. No. No. No. Stop it.

Mum   Sometimes one should just play to one's best attributes and not try to be someone you're not.

Swimmer   Fuck. Stop it.

Mum   Know your strengths. Only disappointment lies in striving for too much. Believe me. My mother taught me that and she was right. She wasn't right about a lot of things but she was right about that. Pass me some water will you, my mouth is dry.

Swimmer   What?

Mum   Or some of the ice you got. I'll have some ice chips. It's no good pretending we're not different. That we don't have different physiques. That we're not as strong as them. We're built to do different things. To carry children. To birth them. To nurture. We have different requirements, as do they. There's no use in pretending this isn't so. Why fight such things? Accept them. And find your strengths within it. It's such a massive waste of everyone's time trying to pretend we're all the same.

Swimmer　I've never said we're the same.

Mum　Banging on about equality. It's an impossible ask. Stop asking it. Find something more productive to do. After all look at your sister.

Swimmer　I can't talk to you about this.

Mum　Well when is, for godsake? It's not like I'm going anywhere. Her curse literally killed her.

Swimmer　Not now. Now isn't the time.

Mum　She battled admirably but what can one do?

Swimmer　Focus on the swim stroke. Focus on your arms.

Mum　Oh ignore me. OK.

Swimmer　You have to have a wider position with your arms and where your hands meet the water when you're in open water.

Mum　Pathetic.

The **Swimmer** *is clearly affected by the presence of her* **Mum***.*

Swimmer　It's not like swimming in a pool. Stability. Strength. And you use your legs less. Your legs are mostly keeping you afloat. It's your arms and shoulders providing the power. The speed. Which makes sense really because they're the ones up front. In charge of progress.

Mum　I'll tell you progress. Progress is acceptance that there will be no progress. Not truly. There never will be. Because this will be the eternal struggle of us all. For ever. As it ever has been. Acceptance. For when I'm gone you will also need to learn acceptance. Because really nothing is in our control, nothing can be changed, nothing can be stopped. And you will learn this when I'm gone. She had so much pain and no one would listen to her and no one would do anything and it defeated her. Sometimes things are just too big for us. This is too big for you.

The **Swimmer** *recites the first three lines of Pablo Neruda's poem 'The Sea'.*

That's Pablo Neruda.

I think that when you lose something you can spend a lot of time thinking about what came before and the moment of it happening but you don't spend enough time looking at after.

The feeding pole and water bottle appear and she drinks and eats.

They've stopped giving me jelly babies. Only carb drink. They must be trying to shorten my feeds. Why? Shit. Am I not swimming fast enough?

Mum   The problem is that you get so defensive all the time. I only say these things out of love for you. It's all coming from a loving place. I don't want to see you hurt.

Swimmer   How is it going to see me hurt?

Mum   It's you that's always so miserable.

Swimmer   I'm not always.

Mum   Well perhaps next time you are crying about how you feel or look or something someone has said or done, perhaps don't come to me again then? Because I clearly don't help you. I clearly don't know how to say the right things.

Swimmer   Now you're being defensive.

Mum   Well I just never know how to be around you. For godsake. I mean. For godsake.

Swimmer   Try maybe not focusing on my body.

Mum   You have big bones like me. It means you carry weight easier but you appear heavier set.

Swimmer   Thanks.

Mum   Just stating the facts.

Swimmer   I know the facts.

Mum   It's a dreadful affliction. Your grandmother was the same. The whole family on her side were. Women with bigger features. It's why I lumber, why I'm lumbering.

Swimmer   You're not lumbering.

Mum   I am. It's what my sister said to me once and it's stuck. It's true. And you are too.

Swimmer   The thing is that this is a solitary endeavor. Yes? It's solitary.

Mum *leaves.*

Swimmer (*firm*)   This is nothing to do with her now. She has no right to all this now. This is mine. And actually I can't do this if she's going to be here. So she needs to stay right out of this and leave me be. Actually. OK?

She looks around and sees **Mum** *isn't around. She focuses on swimming. The white board appears again 'You're doing amazing! Not long till the sun comes up'. The feeding pole and bottle comes down. She drinks. And eats.*

Swimmer   The saltwater is hurting my skin now. My lips feel strange. And I can feel my shoulder starting to twinge. I have an old injury from way back that has always been a worry. And I knew it would give me a hard time but I was hoping it wouldn't do it so soon. I think I'm making good time though. Just got to keep my pace steady.

Mum   I never really understood you two when you were together. You used to be a whole different kind of creature. Speaking your own language. Laughing. Cackling. It was completely frustrating being around you both. She depended on you though. More than you on her. She needed you. I couldn't understand it. She was a much better swimmer than you too.

Swimmer *keeps swimming. Trying to ignore* **Mum**.

Mum   She was much better than you at lots of things.

Mum *seems to shift in time somehow. Her words coming from different memories.*

Why don't you want to come around?

Another shift.

Will you both just stop fucking around. Just stop being such little shits. Just stop. For fucksake.

Another shift.

If you even took half a moment to look at yourself you'd understand why no one will ever want to make you happy.

Another shift.

She got the looks and you got the brains. Not that you're doing anything with them. Other than taking after your old mum. You stick with me; we can be nothing together.

Another shift.

If only we didn't live in a world that valued the beauty of a woman so highly. I feel like we could have been much happier, you and I. I feel like we could have lived better lives. But the world isn't like that and this is our lot. Stomach in and shoulders out. At least create the illusion that you care. Misery is genetic my dear. You should never have chosen me as your mother.

Another shift.

(*In distress.*) Oh god, oh god, oh god.

Swimmer   I wish you weren't here.

Mum   But I am. Fucking deal with it.

Swimmer   This is my swim.

Mum   No it isn't, it was hers.

Swimmer   It has to be mine.

Mum   I have no idea why you always insist on setting yourself up for such massive failures. You seem hell bent on self destruction.

Swimmer   Please go.

Mum   Make me.

Swimmer   This is hard enough as it is.

Mum   So stop.

Swimmer   I can't.

Mum   Yes you can. You're good at stopping. You're good at quitting things. When you were five you quit ballet because you found it too hard. You tried about ten different instruments and didn't last more than a few lessons for each. The money I spent on that fucking oboe. You've never held onto a job for longer than a few years. This is what you do. No one will be surprised. You've impressed everyone by trying to do this. You can stop now. So stop.

Swimmer   Is this what I will have to endure if I continue?

Mum   I'm not going anywhere. Much like you.

Swimmer   I am going to do this.

Mum   You don't sound very sure. Why don't you have a break and think about it? I've found that often just letting go of everything and letting yourself start again helps. When I found myself a single mother of two, no money, living in some dingy one bed flat in the middle of nowhere in some godawful town with no friends or family do you know what I did? Nothing. I sat in that flat and waited.

Swimmer   I remember.

Mum   There was nothing for me outside so I waited until there was. And when there wasn't for a while I waited some more. And eventually with them two going to school and seasons changing and the world revolving, things started to slowly rectify themselves and all was fine. You see? Not everything needs action. Not everything demands an aggressive assault. Perhaps you're simply trying too hard.

Swimmer (*urgently*)   You were the one who taught me to swim in the first place. And you were the one that first took us swimming outside. Not in a swimming pool. A river. Which one? Where was it? Don't remember it being much of a drive. It wasn't a particularly nice day but maybe that's why you chose it because there were only a couple of other people there on the banks. On a hot day it was probably busier. You brought us both but she wasn't old enough yet, was she even crawling? I don't remember. She must have just laid on a rug while we went in. I remember the way in was down the bank and feet into the shallows. Sinking into the mud. Sludge between my toes. Grit and sticks. Feeling it pressing under my toe nails. Looking up at you holding my hand. Still amazed at seeing you in just a swimming costume. So used to only ever seeing you with all your layers. You holding my hand and guiding me in. Despite the cold I was excited wasn't I? Wading out. Up to my bum. Arms raised up above my chest, panting with the chill. Laughing. 'Be quick, don't change your mind' you said. And in. Quick strokes in circles. Raising myself up so I can look beneath, checking for monsters. Half in love with it half terrified. Cold and unknown. And with you. And you're in. And it's just your head I can see and the rest is submerged and you're smiling. Because no one can see your form but also because it just feels so fantastic. And you're panting too. But you're laughing. And whooping. Yes you whooped. God you were happy. I'd never seen you so happy. You were never like this at home.

The feeding pole and water bottle appears again. She drinks and feeds treading water. They go. She doesn't resume swimming. She has stalled.

Mum   She said the swimming helped the pains.

Swimmer   Yes.

Mum   But not enough.

Swimmer   No.

Mum   You can't do anything suddenly in water. You can't do anything quickly. Even great big rocks take time to sink. When you were ten years old and she was five we went to the south west point of Wales do you remember? We camped. The weather was filthy. We spent most of the trip driving round in the car with the windows steamed up and listening to *Under Milk Wood* on the stereo. I bought you a little learn-to-knit kit and you sat in the back seat knitting a long scarf for your doll. We would try and light the fire to cook tea then give up and go to the local pub for chips. Do you remember?

Swimmer   Yes.

Mum   There was that one day, and the weather cleared up for a few hours and we went to the beach. We had to walk down a cliff path for about twenty minutes but when we got there we had the most incredible huge sandy beach with these enormous monolithic stones jutting out all around. And at the base of each one were the most magical rock pools, some deep enough for you to swim in. And the sea was as flat as a mill pond and the most beautiful sapphire blue. Crystal. And the three of us had this wonderful beach to ourselves so we took off all our clothes and we ran into the sea. You were so unselfconscious. You were so free. And so was I. In that one moment. It was soon after the split. It was my turn for a holiday with you both. I was going through a strange time.

Swimmer   You'd never been naked in front of us before then. I remember this so much. Why is this coming to me now? Didn't some family come down the path? Didn't we have to run for our clothes? You made us go back to the car after. We didn't want to go back yet but you were too embarrassed.

Mum   It wasn't always bad. You've stopped. Probably best.

Swimmer   No!

She starts swimming again.

Mum *goes.*

Swimmer   Come on come on come on! Back in it. Back in it.

She hard swims for a bit.

OK fine. OK. This is what it needs to be to do this? Fine. I can do this. And her. This is fine. Let's fucking do this.

She swims hard.

10: Fish and chips. 9: Spag-Bol. 8: Chicken and roast potatoes. 7: Cheese and tomato sandwiches. Fresh, not for packed lunch, because by the time you ate them they were soggy. 6: Cheese and pickle sandwiches are much better at surviving till lunch. 5: Treacle tart. 4: Sushi. 3: Ramen. 2: Pizza. 1: Bits and pieces. Which is the Sunday evening meal in front of the telly. Just whatever she had in the fridge. Cheese, carrots, apple, bread and butter, maybe some sandwich spread, olives and tomatoes, ham. Best meal ever. We were good at eating. But we also knew how to feel guilty about it when we did. That was Mum's best lesson.

The food and water appear again. She eats and drinks as before.

You can't do anything *quickly* in water. That's what she would say. Not Mum. Mum stole it from her. It was something she loved about swimming. And she was better than me that's true. And she was stronger, even though she was smaller. She had a flow to her. She was fast. But even when you're fast you can't go at speed through water. Particularly not one with currents. With the weather changing at every moment. With nothing but you and your body propelling you. Nothing but flesh. And flesh can be so unreliable.

She swims.

The thing about loss is that there are often so many opportunities to have prevented it. And there are often no opportunities at all.

They were both so much stronger than me always. My sister was just built strong. I'm big but I've always seemed weaker. But her mind was softer. She worried too much. She listened to Mum too much. About herself. Not when she was out in the water though. Maybe because she was so sure of her body when she was in the sea. Of her body's ability. So she didn't need to worry. Maybe because the water soothed her. That strong body of hers enduring that pain so much better than I would have been able to.

And I think of her when she used to not care what others thought. And her laughing. When did she lose that? Who took that from her? Or was it just the long queue of people who didn't help her that did it? The doctor whose face changed when she said why she was writhing in agony; who suddenly didn't take her as seriously; who forgot to put through the request for morphine because she wasn't a priority anymore. Or the junior doctor who actually laughed when she said it was her period and asked if she'd tried taking an ibuprofen. Or the countless women who just couldn't understand why she struggled with it so much when they didn't. Or women who said 'you got to try giving birth – now that's true pain'. Or all the jobs she stuffed up with time off or by putting in a crappy day's work because she could barely see with it. Or when she was fired for not turning up one day because she'd passed out on the street and been rushed to hospital. All these times. All these times. Because of a period. A fucking period. And once it's over and you can breathe again you know you've only got a month or less to go until it all starts again. How can that not break a person down?

Just focus on your breathing. Focus on your stroke.

*The **Swimmer** recites lines 21 and 22 of Pablo Neruda's poem 'The Sea'.*

The gradual wearing away of the star.

I had to really talk myself round about the sea. The deep sea. There's something about being out in the middle of it and looking down between strokes at the sea floor disappearing from view as you get further out until you're just looking at the deep dark blue. Or murky brown. And you can't see what's below you. Though you know there has to be so much below you. And you have to do everything in your power not to constantly imagine something coming up from the deep. So much that it takes all of me to keep my eyes open when I put my face in the water. Because I'm so scared of seeing something that I can't do anything about. And yet, here's the crazy bit; I'm also looking. Every breathe I take isn't just to propel myself forwards, it's so I can look. Just in case I see something. And in all my training swims it became mind over matter of dealing with the deep and talking myself through it. And I wondered how I would be once I got out in the channel and would I freak out? Because what else is down there? Creatures?

Relics. Wrecks. All the many many crossings. The people. The boats. The desperation and the fear and the terrible terrible losses. Those people. How many are down there right now? And here I am doing this.

She takes a moment to let that settle.

So I can't look away. I must not look away. But I can feel myself on the edge. The deepness. It's always been. It's always. In the year before she went when she would take me on her swims she would talk me through them. She was so brave. Or perhaps she was just being brave because it was needed. In those moments. Maybe she was just as scared as me. She just taught me not to stop. You have to keep going. You have to power on forwards. Because you're already too far from the shore you left and every stroke takes you closer to the shore in front. Keep fucking swimming. And don't think about what's underneath.

Mum   She used to call me you know? To cry. She felt enormous pressure from you.

Swimmer   About what?

Mum   To be better. She felt like you disapproved of her. That you thought she was making bad decisions. I mean she was right wasn't she? You've never been one to hide your opinions. You can be very judgemental when you want to be. It's so hard living up to the standards you set and your poor sister didn't stand a chance.

Swimmer   I'm judgemental?

Mum   Yes I know it's something you've learnt from me. I'm not a fucking idiot. But I have subtlety.

Swimmer   You have never been subtle.

Mum   Say what you like I have class about it. I know how best to deliver it. You have always come crashing into situations like a great bull with a sore head. Oh my god the times I've wanted to cover your mouth with my hands and drag you out of a room. Your poor sister never stood a chance. And she idolised you. That's why it meant so much to her. That's why it hurt so much.

Swimmer   This is all a bit much actually.

Mum   Sometimes the truth is useful.

Swimmer   Not right now.

Mum   One must face up to one's actions eventually.

Swimmer   Not now.

Mum   Well when you're ready I'll be right here.

Swimmer   I wish you wouldn't. Can't you just leave me to do this on my own?

Mum   Well then it wouldn't be a challenge would it?

Swimmer   I think swimming the fucking channel is challenge enough with you looking over my shoulder trying to make me feel like shit. The sea is enough of a fucking challenge.

Mum   This is nothing to do with the sea, my dear.

Swimmer   Yes it is, of course it is.

Mum   Well keep swimming then.

Swimmer   I will!

Mum   Keep swimming if you can.

She goes. White board – 'Look out for the sun!' The food and water appear again. **Swimmer** *eats and drinks.*

Swimmer   How many hours is that now? How many miles? I'm losing count. Focus on your arms. Focus. Oh!

The sun is rising. She watches as the light changes around her.

I worry about having a daughter myself. I don't trust I'll get it right.

This is getting harder now. I did one of my training swims on Lake Windermere as it's a good chance to do one long stretch that is similar and actually it's harder as it's fresh water so you don't have the buoyancy that the sea gives you. It's a good practice. And it's hard. But I'm beginning to feel it now. It's one long push all the

way to France. My shoulders are beginning to ache and the wind
has picked up a bit so every now and then I get a wave in the face
and I've been swallowing water. This isn't good because it
probably means I'll be throwing up before long. This is hard.
Swimming was my sister's thing. I made it mine for her. Setting
out together. Striking for the other side of the bay. Making
thermoses of hot tea and sandwiches for after and going in search
of hidden lagoons in rivers and new sections of coast. It was the
one thing that would keep her mood up. I used to make sure she
went. It was something practical I could actually do. And since she
. . . I mean since she . . . after she had gone I found myself still
striking out. On my own. And every time I hit the cold water I
would feel again. It made me feel.

'I must go down to the seas again

To the lonely sea and sky.'

We needed each other as much as we didn't.

I did believe her, I did believe her, I did believe her.

They put her under a general anaesthic to look inside and work out
what was going on. They were thinking maybe endometriosis or
polycystic ovaries. That way, once they'd diagnosed it, they could
treat it and hopefully help her manage the pain better. But after
knocking her out and having a good old rummage in there they
found nothing. Nothing at all. I've never seen her so crushed.
There was nothing to explain this pain. And everything anyone had
ever said about it being some kind of invention or some kind of
exaggeration suddenly came home. She had hoped to prove
everyone wrong. Why had they found nothing?

I did believe her. Even if she thought I didn't.

There are two things that can make me cry. Stubbing my toe and
'Kissing You' by Des'ree from the soundtrack of Baz Luhrmann's
Romeo + Juliet. I don't know what it is but there is some kind of
Pavlovian fucking response going on there. My 1999 heartbreaker
took me to see this fucking film and then broke up with me and
that fucking song is so full of strings and surging and the piano and

oh god I don't fucking know but it makes me cry so fucking much. Just thinking about it now and I'm going. Don't do this don't do this. It'll fuck my breathing. Don't do this. Stop it. Stupid fucking Des'ree.

Shit.

She swims hard for a bit.

I can't cry because I'm already surrounded by water.

The water and food drops down again. She feeds. It goes. **Mum** *arrives and sings a section of the 'Swimming Song' by Loudon Wainwright.*

Swimmer   I wish you'd go.

Mum   Hop up on the boat now. You've done all you can.

Swimmer   I haven't. And I'm fine. It's you that's exhausting me.

Mum   Yes you're exhausted. There's no point killing yourself just to make a point. Find your sensible head. Up on the boat now.

Swimmer   No.

Mum   If you listen to your instincts they will be screaming at you to be safe.

Swimmer   Stop this.

Mum   Not until I know you're OK.

Swimmer   I am OK. I was. Leave me alone and I'll be better.

Mum   Up on the boat.

Swimmer   No.

Mum   Out you get.

Swimmer   No.

Mum   It's probably for the best now anyway.

Swimmer   Why?

Mum   Because you've missed your window.

Swimmer   What?

Mum   You were going too slow weren't you? So now you've missed the tide.

Swimmer   No I haven't.

Mum   Yes you have. They're about to let you know.

Swimmer   No they aren't. Shut up. Stop fucking with my head. I can't miss the window.

Mum   Well you have.

Swimmer   I can't!

The white board 'You've missed the window. The tide has turned. Keep going. You can do it'.

No. Oh god. Oh no.

Mum   What's that then? Another six hours? Eight? On top of what you are doing anyway. Will that make it an eighteen hour swim? Twenty?

Swimmer   No no no.

Mum   Of course you missed the window. It wouldn't be right without a bit of drama from you, would it?

Swimmer   Fuck you! FUCK YOU! You made this happen! You fucking horrible bitch!

Mum   Me? How would I control the tides?

Swimmer   You slowed me down!

Mum   Do I control your limbs?

Swimmer   You horrible horrible . . . fuck you! I don't believe this. Oh god I can't believe this.

Mum   Your sister wouldn't have missed the window.

Swimmer   Shut up!

Mum   I'm just saying what you're thinking.

Swimmer   But why? Why?

Mum   You have such a selective memory.

Swimmer   I don't.

Mum   You do. Why are you remembering me like this?

Swimmer   Stop talking! Stop! I have to sort my head. I have to get my head round this. ohgodohgodohgod.

She swims for a concentrated amount of time. Her limbs seem heavier. She is slow and plodding at first. She manages to pick up her speed and look determined.

If it's to be more hours then that's it then. I'm still in the water. I'm still in the water. It's words. I feel weighed down by all the words. Why do we keep saying them?

Mum   I think you're tired. You're no longer making much sense.

Swimmer   I am. I am making sense. Why did no one believe her? It's like everything. It's like everything, isn't it? What we say, what is said to us; we aren't to be believed, we aren't to be taken seriously, we aren't a priority. It's like someone has tied all those words used to describe, to hurt, to attack, to compliment, to belittle, to disarm, to ignore and they've tied them all to our ankles. With a chain. And they've thrown us in the water. And we are expected to keep afloat. In the same water they're in. This fucking swim. It's everything. It's just too far, isn't it? Oh god oh god. It's just too far. What did she say? What did she say? 'One kick at a time'. Yes.

She swims.

10: 'Like a girl'. 9: Pussy. 8: Cow. 7: Whore. 6: Bitch – why is it that when you call a woman a bitch it's because she's been aggressive or strong or assertive but when you call a man one it's because he's pathetic, weak or useless? You can't have it both ways. 5: Slut. 4: Tit. 3: Twat. 2: Slag. 1: Cunt. Top ten. For me anyway.

The water and food appears again.

Swimmer *breathes for a moment or two.*

(*Trying to focus herself.*) 'I must go down to the seas again, for the call of the running tide

Is a wild call and a clear call that may not be denied.'

The food and water bottle appear again. She feeds.

(*Urgently.*) My sister had this story of a time at school when she liked some boy. And this boy was the one everyone liked. And her best friend was talking to him and they were laughing and looking at her. And when she asked her friend what they were laughing about she was told, and I mean it's so fucking infantile, it's so fucking pathetic and why would anyone be bothered by this but I mean they were laughing because he had described her as a hairy gorilla. And she told me this story quite late on. She'd been hanging onto it. She had been ashamed of this. That this was how she'd been described. And she said that after that she went home and shaved her legs. And shaved her pubic hair. And her underarm. She shaved everything. Her beautiful, newly womanly body, became bare and scraped smooth. And even later, when she was older, when she was less bothered, she still felt weird about having hair on her body. She once had an unexpected one night stand where she got back to the guy's house and insisted on being allowed to shave her legs because she didn't want to get into his bed hairy. She didn't feel sexy enough. It didn't matter this guy was three fucking sheets to the wind and wouldn't have noticed let alone cared if he was worth anything at all. Do you see? Do you see what I mean?

Mum   Have you spoken to your sister recently?

Swimmer   The other day, why?

Mum   She's broken up with the latest one. She was hysterical.

Swimmer   When?

Mum   Yesterday. I told her it was good riddance.

Swimmer   She didn't call.

Mum   She was worried you'd say I told you so.

Swimmer   Really?

Mum   Of course she was.

Swimmer   I'll call her now.

Mum   You didn't though did you?

Swimmer   I was going to that evening. I wanted to call her when I could actually talk for longer than five minutes.

Mum   No good now.

Swimmer   Please.

Food and drink.

Mum   She couldn't. I couldn't. It's OK not to.

Swimmer   I wanted to do it.

Mum   I was a fat child.

Swimmer   What?

Mum   I was active but I was fat.

Swimmer   Mum please.

Mum   And it meant that I was often remarked upon. Mostly by my mum. She was very good at letting me know in her round about way that I wasn't the right shape. Insidious stuff. 'Are you sure you want seconds?' 'Now then, you shouldn't be eating that.' 'My little pigpig.' 'No wonder you keep growing out of your clothes.' I was her fat child. I used to do ballet. It was all I wanted to do but I didn't look like the other girls in my tutu. And they made sure I knew that. I so wanted to do ballet. Desperately so. But I was so aware that my body wasn't right for it. I was not the right physique. I was pointed in the direction of lacrosse I think. I chose to swim.

Swimmer   Odd choice really.

Mum   Why?

Swimmer   You have to wear very little. Expose your body.

Mum   But once you're in.

Swimmer   Yes.

Mum   Nothing more liberating. Am I dying?

Swimmer   Yes, Mum.

Mum   Oh.

Swimmer   I think you're doing it pretty well though.

Mum   What's that supposed to mean?

Swimmer   I don't know. Didn't know what else to say.

Mum   I was watching a documentary. Where's it gone?

Swimmer   You asked for the telly off.

Mum   It was about freak waves. Terrifying. Though I'd be amazed if you get anything like that in the channel.

Swimmer   . . .

Mum   You heard about your booking yet? You got a boat?

Swimmer   I have but I don't think I can take it.

Mum   Yes you can. She would have wanted that.

Swimmer   I've not trained enough. Not to do it this year. And it all feels pointless now anyway.

Mum   Pathetic.

Swimmer   Alright.

Mum   Stupid.

Swimmer   OK, Mum, calm down. Do you want the telly on again?

Mum   A freak wave isn't like a tsunami wave where it's triggered by a big event like an earthquake. Instead it's the culmination of lots of smaller waves all just coming together at one time. It's the collection of them all and their energy that suddenly creates this big wave out of nowhere. A completely random event. Something scientists can't predict. In fact they didn't even believe it was true until recently. Until they could observe them. Just sailors' tales of 100-foot waves.

Swimmer   Why are you telling me this?

Mum   Chaos. Random.

Swimmer   Mum, do you need to rest?

Mum   All these small things.

Swimmer   Yes.

Mum   You are going to do it aren't you?

Swimmer   Do what?

Mum   Swim.

Swimmer   Yes, Mum.

Mum   Every stroke.

Swimmer   Rest now, Mum.

Mum   Keep focusing on your stroke.

The water and food appears again. She drinks. She eats. She vomits.

Swimmer   No. Nope. Oh shit this is too hard. I can't do this. How many miles left? Anyone? Just shout it! I can't read what you've written. I can't hear over the engine! Hold your fingers up. How many miles? Is that how many I've done or how many I've got left? Tell me how many I've got left. Why not? Oh fuck it. Am I making progress? Yes? OK thank you. Thank you!

Oh god come on. COME ON.

She swims. A sense of intensity and no thoughts.

Focus. On. Your. Stroke.

Swimmer *is feeling incredibly tired by her swim now.*

Swimmer   Drowning. Drowning. Facts: Drowning. Nearly 80 per cent of people who drown are male. Mainly because of proximity to water through their jobs, or drinking near water or stuff like swimming alone or boating. Those are accidents though. Not. Not. It's fast and silent. It can take only twenty seconds. Drowning in salt water takes longer. Something to do with the salt saturation and blood. Usually takes eight to ten minutes. Which means that rescuing people in the sea is more likely than in fresh water. Which is why I . . . which is why it . . . Also it doesn't look like you'd think. Not the splashing, arms flailing, shouting you see on screen. Just head bobbing. Just panicked eyes. I think, beyond that, they say there is a kind of euphoria. That people who have been revived after nearly drowning have sometimes been angry because they felt so happy. Beyond the first bit, after the straining for breath, there's some kind of peace. It would be hard for a person to do it to themself though wouldn't it? Would need to maybe weigh yourself down? Stones maybe. How would someone do it way out in the middle of the ocean? Without an overwhelming swell to do it for you? A storm. How would you do it? And really is it euphoric or is it actually just really fucking terrifying? Like are your final moments beautiful or filled with absolute horror and panic and pain? What does it feel like? What would it be like? Oh fuck oh fuck oh fuck.

She's struggling. She's hit her wall.

I could just ask to get on the boat. I could just abort. I could just stop right now. Why the fuck don't I? Why the fuck don't I? Why the fuck don't I just stop?

The water and food drop down again.

Mum   When I had you and your sister I realised many things.

Swimmer   No. OK? No. I can't. I have to just focus on my stroke. This isn't helping me.

Mum   I realised many things.

Swimmer   I said no.

Mum   I realised many things. The first was that I wasn't as good at it as I thought I would be. It was hard. Getting things right. I think you always think that when you come to have children of your own you will know what to do. That when you've observed others and their children you've seen the mistakes they've made. You can easily see from the outside in. And I think you assume that you won't make those mistakes. Or you would handle things better. And also that you would just know what to do when the time came because they are your children. You will know what to do with your children.

Swimmer   Mum, you're tired. I don't think you should be speaking so much.

Mum   I was so hard on your grandmother. For the way she raised me.

Swimmer   It sounded like you were right to be.

Mum   And you would be right to be hard on me.

Swimmer   Look we don't need to do this now.

Mum   You think I was a bad mother.

Swimmer   . . .

Mum   Your sister does too.

Swimmer   Mum, you're tired.

Mum   It's just words. It's all just words.

Swimmer   Stopthinkingstopthinkingstopthinking.

Swimmer *tries to focus entirely on her swimming over the following.*

Mum *recites the last ten lines of Pablo Neruda's poem 'The Sea'.*

Swimmer   That's Neruda again. 'I became part of it's pure movement.' I didn't call my sister and at that moment when I didn't call her they think that it was about the time that she left her clothes on the beach and walked over the shingle into the sea. About the time when she pushed through the breaking waves and front crawled out. Beyond the white horses crashing to the shore. Beyond the rip. Did she look back at the cliffs? Did she look back at all or did she just plough on? She was headed in the direction of France at least. But she wasn't making a crossing attempt. She just wanted to get far enough out so no one could see her. The lifeguard had seen her go in but didn't realise she wasn't back until the beach was clearing at the end of the day and no one was claiming the little pile of clothes with no towel. No towel. Of course she didn't bring a towel because she wouldn't need it. Oh. Oh. OH. NO! No mumma no! I can't. I can't. Mamma I can't.

She has slowed right down. **Mum** *is watching.* **Swimmer** *is holding back sobs and not letting herself cry.*

Swimmer   I can't.

Suddenly . . .

Oh fuck is that?

She is suddenly frozen in the water, looking down. She looks back up.

Shit. No not now.

She looks down again, checking. She looks back up. Panicked.

Fucking JELLIES. I can see shit load of jellies. Too many. Too many. Too many to swim round. Fuck. Fuck. OW. OW. NO!

She screams out in pain. She is being stung very badly. She screams. Voices call from the boat. They discernibly are trying to tell her to keep swimming to get through the cloud. She swims but is in a lot of pain. Eventually she slows and looks down again. Satisfied she resumes swimming.

Gone. Passed. I did it. I did it. Oh god it hurts.

She looks up at the boat. They are shouting to her to come in. She shouts back.

I'm OK! I think. MAMA I DID IT! Are you still anywhere? Are you still there?

Mum   I'm here.

Swimmer   Did you see that? Did you see?

Mum   Yes love.

Swimmer   It hurts, Mum.

She struggles to keep going. She treads water panting but not crying. The sound of the motor of the support boat. Voices. Indiscernible. Encouraging. Shouting.

The voices continue. Still indiscernable.

Tired.

Mum   'And all I ask is a merry yarn from a laughing fellow-rover, And quiet sleep and a sweet dream when the long trick's over.'

Why have you stopped?

Swimmer   You're not here.

Mum   Don't stop.

Swimmer   You're not here.

Mum   I remember you stumbling through that door. Crying your little heart out. We were so cross with you.

Swimmer   I know. It didn't help. Mum, she was so scared.

Mum   Of what?

Swimmer   Losing you. I was too.

Mum   Why have you stopped?

Swimmer   I can't do this.

Mum   Yes you can. A series of small waves. Completely random.

Swimmer   She's gone, Mum. She's gone. Like you. Both of you. And here I am in the middle of the fucking English Channel doing something I'd never thought I'd ever do. She's gone. Why am I even here? She's gone.

Mum   Look at what you've done. You're nearly there.

Swimmer   I'm not. I can't do it. That's it.

Mum   Look up. Look up. You're almost there

Mum *exits.* **Swimmer** *is pushing as hard as she can now. She's so tired.*

Swimmer   The first woman to do the channel crossing was Gertrude Ederle and she did it using front crawl so she could beat the existing men's record. This was 1926. She beat it by two hours. There are just these people in the world who go out to do incredible things. Feats. Amazing things. Her hearing was permanently affected by the waves. She had nervous breakdowns for the rest of her life. But she swam the fucking Channel. She swam it. During a time when there was no GPS tracking for ferries or your route. When there was no online network of other swimmers to get advice from. To train with. And when there was still only a few people who had done it before. And she was the first woman. Despite everything. I mean she must have had some shit for that. She must have. And she did it. What a fucking adventure. What a feat. To do that with just your body.

You have to get to the beach just south of the Cap Gris-Nez. The boat has to stay about 400 metres out from the shore while you keep swimming, get to the beach and clamber out. You have to get fully out and above the water line for it to be official. Your observers on the boat will be able to confirm this happened. Some have done the whole swim and not quite made it to the right point on the beach. Or not got out properly. Gutting. I mean how gutting would that be? Some say that when they make it they are so exhausted they just want to sit on the beach with their head in their hands. Some manage to jump up and down with fucking elation. Some just laugh. I'm so tired I don't know what I'll do. But there it is. I can see the shore. COME ON!

She pushes harder.

My body. My body. My body did this.

There's a pub in Dover where everyone one who's ever swum the Channel writes their name on the wall. My sister and I had a pint in there one day and that's where she hatched her plan to swim it. We were bracing ourselves for a visit to Mum. We knew Mum was ill.

We knew she was going to tell us she was dying. My sister said to me that if she was then she would swim the Channel for her. She would do it to show her that we were going to be OK. That she didn't need to worry about us anymore. That her daughters were fine. She can't have known then that she would be gone before Mum was. She can't have known then that it would be me writing my name on the pub wall and not her. I feel like I've been stuck in a rip for so long now. I've not stopped hearing the roar of the sea. And I can still hear Mum crying out for me from the shore.

She is nearly there.

So much of our make up is water that when you swim I think it's just like extending yourself. Expanding your body to include the miles and miles of ocean around you. You become part of the waves. Which rise up into being, standing out from the other waves, standing out from the rest of the sea. Before easing down, sometimes crashing down, to rejoin the water they are made of.

She reaches the shore. She climbs out of the water and staggers up the beach. She turns to face the sea and waves at the boat. We hear distant cheers over the sound of the boat's engine. These cut out to silence. The wind. The waves. She is shaking. She is tired. She is alone. She wraps her arms around her head and she cries.

The Passenger

Morgan Lloyd Malcolm

The Passenger was first performed as part of *Deep Night, Dark Night* at the Sam Wanamaker Playhouse at Shakespeare's Globe. The cast included:

Andrius Gaucas
Evelyn Miller
Imogen Doel
Nathalaie Armin
Paul Ready
Tom Stuart

Creative Team

Director: Isabel Marr
Composer: Laura Moody
Stage Manager: Liz Issac
Candle Technician: Camilla Direk
Production Manager: Fay Powell-Thomas

It was revived with the same cast member (Evelyn Miller) and director (Isabel Marr) as part of the first Terrifying Women night at The Golden Goose Theatre in 2021.

This piece is designed to be performed with incredibly low-fi effects and staging. Its original incarnation was at the Sam Wanamaker Theatre at Shakespeare's Globe which only uses candles for lighting. The sound effects were created by stage management banging on walls and walking round the back of the auditorium. The conceit of the actor being just as unaware of the contents of the story means the ride is a shared experience so connection between the audience and actor is important.

The second time we performed it was in a small fringe venue with a basic lighting wash but again we relied on practical effects of someone banging walls backstage.

If you manage to make your audience scream then you've smashed it. If someone faints (like they did in the Wanamaker) then, after checking they're OK, give yourself a massive pat on the back.

It is incredibly fun to do so enjoy it!

Good evening.

The following has been written by Morgan. I am not Morgan. I am [insert name]. However I will be reading as Morgan. She wanted you to just be made aware that everything that follows, though spoken by me the actor, is completely true. Or at least as true as her memory serves her. Because sometimes these things can become distorted or changed by time and what happened, happened a long time ago. Even if she is still feeling the effects of it now. I should also make it clear that I have not read this yet. It is important that this is the first time I've read this. This was Morgan's stipulation.

Are we? Are we good to go? OK. Good. Sorry. We've been having a few technical difficulties which to be honest is kind of funny considering we're in a venue with very few technical bells and whistles. Ha! What's the equivalent of a power cut when you're powered by candles? That. We've been having a few strange things. A few strange things happening. Which if you asked Morgan she would say she's not surprised about that at all and honestly I've been a bit. It's been a bit. Like it's all a bit. Sorry.

Stop.

Are we good? OK. Let's. I'm going to start. Here we go.

Brief pause as she gathers herself and looks at the document she will be reading from. As she is about to start she suddenly looks up at the back of the auditorium as if she heard something. She waits to see if it's anything, and then looks back at the paper. She must not explain this movement and it needs to be short and sharp.

Sometimes when life becomes harder a person can wonder if they are cursed. Or that there is something about them that if they could just shake off then everything would get better. Run smoother. Some people spend their whole lives feeling like this. I would not describe it as a curse, this story I am going to tell you, it's something else. I liken it to driving on your own at night with the sensation that if you looked in your rear view mirror you would see that you have a passenger. Since I was a child I have had a passenger. This is my story.

I was about seven years old when I became interested in dark and strange things. Perhaps it was the dreams I was having. Perhaps it was the serious accident my father had. Perhaps it was the house my grandmother lived in. Because some of the best ghost stories are about scary houses aren't they?

I now know that all of these things were factors but back then I just thought that my brain was there to terrify me at night and that what I needed to do was to try and understand the unexplainable in order to try and make sense of it all.

So I read ghost stories. I read accounts of monsters and ghouls. I wrote them too. I imagined dark and terrible things and wrote them down. I became obsessed with telling stories to my friends that would scare them. Because I knew that if I was the one telling the story then I was in control of the fear.

Because fear is like blood in the water. It attracts the very creatures we are so scared of.

And fear for each of us is so personal. What would push one person to the edge might only thrill another. And yet there are some things we all fear so instinctively that if you have enough people in one place at one time experiencing something collectively . . .

She looks up at everyone briefly.

. . . you cannot control what might happen.

As a child I knew the power of this. It is why when on a school residential trip I was able to convince a whole dormitory of girls that the night before I had seen the ghostly figure of a man outside their window. That he was probably the ghost of someone murdered many years ago who sought vengeance for his untimely death. That it only took an open window for him to interpret an invitation to enter and choose one girl to drag to hell. So convincing was I that after I had returned to my bed in another dormitory I was soon collected by my teacher and ordered to go and tell the twenty or so sobbing girls that I had made it all up and then I was made to stand in the corridor for an hour of penance for my crime.

I learnt at an early age the power of telling a good scary story.

The problem was that my inspiration for such stories had to come from somewhere. And like I mentioned a few things had been happening in my young life that had shifted my view of the world somewhat.

At seven my father had a serious motorcycle accident that he only just survived and would spend years recovering from and the rest of his life disabled. I learnt at seven that my parents could die.

This was when the dreams started.

Dark, out of control, falling, constricted, sinister dreams that I would wake from panting and sweating and crying out for my mother.

This was when I became convinced I was being watched.

Pause to look up and out suddenly at a sound that she seems to hear.

Because when my father had his accident in London we were with my mother at her mother's house in the West Country. My grandmother lived in an Old Vicarage. She had bought it in the seventies with my step-grandfather. They were the first non-church affiliated people to live there. The previous owner had been the vicar of the village church and he had died there.

The story goes that he had a heart attack at the top of the stairs and fell to his doom. My aunt tells a story of sleeping in the room at the top the stairs and waking at dawn to the sound of digging. When she looked out of the window she could see the figure of a man working his spade in the flower beds outside. But as she watched him he slowly disappeared. Vanished into the morning mist. The vicar had been a keen gardener as the story goes.

I've always wondered who else died in that house before him. Because I know who died after. And perhaps it was all the external factors of what I was experiencing with my father's ill health but I was so sure that this man was refusing to leave his home for a reason. Like I said. I felt like I was being watched.

A sharp clatter of some metal objects being knocked off a table and hitting the floor. It startles her. A muffled 'sorry!' comes from back stage. She laughs.

It's OK that was our stage manager [insert name]. Ha. Good timing.

Back to reading.

You see I had been writing dark strange stories about unexplainable things. Perhaps inspired by what my aunt had seen. Perhaps a ghoulish imagination that somehow I was born with. But I wrote. And though of course we know that really we have very little control over terrible things. To children this isn't so certain. Deep down inside me I think that I decided that through some action of my own doing, perhaps through my obsessions with dark things. Through committing them to paper. Somehow I was responsible for what had happened to my dad.

When I was eleven we moved to the country and lived with my gran for a short while. My brother and I were given the room at the top of the stairs to sleep in.

Let me describe it. It was a square room with an old hearth in it. Three windows with box seats underneath. Two single beds on either side. And crucially three creaky steps down into it.

The creakyness of those steps were a comfort as in my nighttime panics I would know that anyone trying to come in the room would not be able to do it without letting me know. It would give me precious seconds to react. The creak was like an intruder alarm. And my brother was in the bed closest to the door so I knew that whilst he was being eaten by whatever monster had come I could make my escape . . .

Anyway. Remember how I said I had felt like I was being watched? Well one night, not long since we had moved in I woke when the rest of the house was asleep and became aware I was not alone.

I very carefully only slightly opened my eyes a crack and saw that standing next to the bed was a figure. It was dark but I could just about make out that it was a man. With my eyes only slightly open I could not make out much of him. His face seemed blank. And even though I don't remember seeing his eyes I knew from how he was standing that he was watching me as I slept. I did not move a muscle.

But as I opened my eyes more I saw him realise I was awake.

He turned and quickly left the room. And as he walked up the steps. They did not creak.

From that moment on it was as if it had been confirmed to me everything I feared. That the dreams were right. That what my aunt had seen was true. That the room at the top of the stairs was probably the last place I should be sleeping. That this house had shadows. That I could see them. And perhaps because I wanted to join up dots - perhaps my father's accident wasn't the cause of these events. Perhaps it happened because of them. Perhaps it happened because of the house. Perhaps it happened because of the man. And perhaps, somehow by writing about them. As a child. Before everything began. I had invited them in.

So I stopped. After that. I did not write. Not about him. Because I believed that if I wrote it down then it would be solid. It would be true. That somehow he would have reached into me. Made my fingers move. I had seen him. But if I wrote him. What more would happen? I couldn't do it. Until now.

She briefly pauses to acknowledge this.

I'm nearly forty now. And my grandmother's house is no longer in the family. We sold it after she died. But what if I told you, that in the years that we did still have it, through my teen years and my twenties. In those years I never shook the feeling that he was still watching me.

Maybe because of another event not long after he stood over me in the dark.

I was sleeping in that same room at the top of the stairs. And again I woke in the night when everyone was asleep. But he wasn't standing over me this time. Instead I had been woken by the sound of someone chopping wood. Thud. Thud. Thud.

This sound was coming from just outside. A lean-to shed against the side of the house contained the wood for the fires and there was indeed a block and axe. But it was past midnight. No one would surely be chopping wood at this time. Thud. Thud. Thud. I listened to it for only a short while before I decided to get up and go to my parents room.

However. Just as I got to the creaky steps out of the room . . . the chopping stopped. So I did too. I listened to see if it would start again but it didn't. I decided to get back into bed.

I got under the covers and pulled them tight to my chin. Just as I shut my eyes . . . the chopping started again. Thud. Thud. Thud.

Immediately I got up and went to the steps. But just as before it stopped as soon as I reached them. Now I assure you that this was beginning to really scare me but part of me wanted to believe that whatever was out of my sight and in a shed on the other side of the wall couldn't possibly be watching my movements. Could it? Could he? Either someone really was chopping wood past midnight and just happened to have stopped and started at the exact time I was getting up and down from bed. Or I was being watched.

I decided to test it one more time. So I went back to the bed and slipped under the covers, bringing them up to my chin. And barely able to breathe I waited. I waited to see if the chopping would start. And. Thud. Thud. Thud.

On the final 'thud' a bang from behind the seating should happen which makes her look up in shock. She waits to hear if they continue for a moment then goes back to reading.

I did not wait. I got up and ran to my parents room. I slept between them that night. I did not utter a word as to why.

It was like he wanted me to know that no matter where I was; he could see me.

I have carried him with me all these years because it felt safer to do that than not. If he is only watching me. Then he will leave my family alone. And if I wrote about him again, like I did before my father's accident, what would happen next?

But life isn't as neat as all that is it? If only it was as simple as that: If I do not write of the man then no harm will come of my loved ones.

For he wasn't the only one to die in that house. Three more people would. My step grandfather. My grandmother. And finally, my father. In the same room where we were woken all those years ago by the phone call to say he was hurt.

The other night I was woken from a dream by someone saying my name. I lay next to my sleeping husband straining my eyes to see through the dark at who it was. I thought I caught a glimpse of something in the glass of a framed print. I stopped breathing when I thought the dressing gown on the back of the door was the figure of a man. It wasn't. But someone had said my name.

Like all the times since my childhood that I had felt a hand on my shoulder. Or thought I heard footsteps upstairs. Or could have sworn there was someone looking at me from the hall. The many, countless moments of pure terror I have felt. Of white, breathless, gut twisting terror. That colours every moment that could otherwise be happy. Calm even. To live every day in fear of what could be. I am so tired. I'm so tired now. My passenger did not need my grandmother's house. He needed me. And he has been watching me all my life.

And perhaps I have no control over it. Or him. Perhaps I was wrong to think that writing about him will change anything. But if it does release him from me somehow. If it does. So that someone else will become his focus. If it works.

I had to try.

And for this I am sorry. To the person reading for me right now.

Take a moment to take that in.

For it is a burden. Fear. And many have it for so many reasons. But this one is so personal to me and I don't want it anymore.

I hope this works. And we will only know if it has if he shows you he is watching. So reader, please stand.

She stands, nervous.

And wait. Then very slowly raise your hand, as if you are reaching for the door. And if he is watching you then . . .

Three loud bangs from behind the audience. She screams.

End.

www.ingramcontent.com/pod-product-compliance
Ingram Content Group UK Ltd.
Pitfield, Milton Keynes, MK11 3LW, UK
UKHW020716280225
455688UK00012B/389